ENDORSEMENTS

Awakening Your Prophetic Voice by Betsy Jacobs is an incredibly powerful and practical tool for every believer to personally connect with the voice of God for themselves. This is not just another book on how to prophesy over others, but rather an intimate guidebook into incorporating the prophetic into your own personal conversations with God.

Through vulnerable, raw, and often funny storytelling, Betsy shares from her own personal journey to impart revelation on both the prophetic and identity. This book is packed with inspiring stories that will keep you turning pages, and practical activation for incorporating the prophetic into your life as a daily practice. If you're a believer who waits on prophetic words from others, then this book will activate you into an exciting adventure and partnership to hear the Lord's voice intimately for yourself, know who He has called you to be, and walk in His wisdom into your destiny!

KRIS VALLOTTON
Leader, Bethel Church, Redding, CA
Co-Founder of Bethel School of Supernatural Ministry
Author of thirteen books, including *The Supernatural Ways of Royalty, Heavy Rain* and *Poverty, Riches and Wealth*

I often assess the value of a story by how it challenges me to a higher level of living in Christ. Betsy's story is both instructional and challenging. She writes authentically, candidly, and full of the passion God has place in her heart for others to hear the voice of God for themselves. I love it when I see God blend his heart with the unique makeup of one of his children resulting in a fresh expression of his thinking through them. As I read Betsy's story I could hear the agelong desire in the heart of God once again being echoed through his servant Moses, *"I wish that all the Lord's people were prophets and that the Lord would put his Spirit on them."* We now live in the realization of this cry. Take up Betsy's challenge to step into your prophetic destiny!

DAVID SMITH
Life Development Coach, Coach Trainer, and Director of
Bethel Coaching at Bethel Church in Redding, Ca
www.coachingin3d.com

I have known Betsy Jacobs for six years and have always enjoyed her personality and communication style. It is honest, and filled with humor and wisdom. If she is going to write, then of course I knew that these are the same traits her readers will experience. I really enjoyed reading her new book, and I know you will too. I highly recommend Betsy Jacob's work to you.

DR. JONATHAN WELTON
President of Welton Academy
www.weltonacademy.com

Betsy Jacobs invites you to awaken and activate a gift that the Holy Spirit has placed within every single believer—the prophetic voice. You have the ability to discern what God says about you, declare/prophesy it over your life, and start stepping into that destiny!

Over the last 20 to 30 years, it has been refreshing to see a renewal in the operation of the gifts of Holy Spirit in the church. This has been especially true concerning prophecy and prophetic ministry. How far we've come! At one point, the mention of the word "prophet" brought to mind images of fire-breathing, over-zealous preachers, glaring around the room looking for sins to expose and saints to shame. By God's grace, that stigma has been demolished and a new standard has been raised up.

Betsy is a voice that God is presently using and will amplify to help a generation discover its own prophetic voice. Not everyone can get called out in a church gathering and receive a destiny-defining prophetic word. We celebrate the times this does happen, sure. But for you, the reader, if you never had someone else give you a prophetic word, I believe it's possible for you to prophesy destiny over yourself. You can give yourself a prophetic word—a word from Heaven that calls your real identity in Christ forth! You can position yourself for a prophetic encounter with the Holy Spirit! And this is where Betsy comes in. As a spiritual coach. As a mentor. As a friend. As someone who shares out of her own experience and testimony, Betsy's refreshingly honest and non-religious writing will engage your mind while, at the same time, awaken your spirit to your prophetic identity in God.

I love her statement: "Many of us want to hear what God has to say about our future, but we aren't willing to do anything with the vision outside of being entertained by it." God gives us prophetic words; however, we are responsible for partnering with them. God sees us a certain way; we need to learn how to agree with His opinion, for God's opinion about you is absolute fact! So get ready for something new and fresh from an emerging voice. I believe this easy-to-use mentoring tool will show you how to position yourself to receive prophetic words from the Lord, release them over your life, and partner with them so that your true identity in Christ comes forth and shapes your destiny!

LARRY SPARKS, MDIV.
Publisher, Destiny Image
Author of *Breakthrough Faith,* co-author of *The Fire That Never Sleeps* with Dr. Michael Brown and John Kilpatrick
Lawrencesparks.com

I could not put this book down and you will not be able to either. As one of Betsy Jacob's pastors I have personally witnessed and benefited from the fruit of her ministry. Betsy has put on paper what has been in her heart for years. You too will benefit from her easy to read personal accounts and practical exercises to help you receive personal revelation from God's heart for you and others. Too many people are living off of second and third hand revelation. This book is exactly what the Body of Christ needs in this hour. Put on your seatbelt and hang on for the ride!

JAY BEAN
Lead Pastor of Grace Church, Springfield, Mo

AWAKENING YOUR PROPHETIC VOICE

AWAKENING

CALLING FORTH YOUR

YOUR

IDENTITY THROUGH

PROPHETIC

PROPHETIC ENCOUNTERS

VOICE

WITH THE HOLY SPIRIT

BETSY JACOBS

DESTINY IMAGE® PUBLISHERS, INC.

P.O. Box 310, Shippensburg, PA 17257-0310

"Promoting Inspired Lives."

This book and all other Destiny Image and Destiny Image Fiction books are available at Christian bookstores and distributors worldwide.

Cover design by Eileen Rockwell

Interior design by Terry Clifton

For more information on foreign distributors, call 717-532-3040.

Reach us on the Internet: www.destinyimage.com.

ISBN 13 TP: 978-0-7684-1878-1

ISBN 13 eBook: 978-0-7684-1879-8

ISBN 13 HC: 978-0-7684-1881-1

ISBN 13 LP: 978-0-7684-1880-4

For Worldwide Distribution, Printed in the U.S.A.

1 2 3 4 5 6 7 8 / 22 21 20 19 18

DEDICATION

To Ben Jacobs

For our children's children. Together.

ACKNOWLEDGMENTS

I would like to thank my teachers—Mom and Dad, Ben Jacobs, Daniel Banks, Jonathan and Karen Welton, Ben Valence, Terry Wiegand, and Jay Bean. You have been a direct influence, a source of encouragement, and a constructive guide for this work.

Also, my very first class from which this devotional was birthed—thank you Christy Berryman, Fran Ellsaesser, Jennifer Jacobs, Tiffany Goodin, Doug and Terry Wiegand, Stefanie Beck, Lorella Moss, Connie Walker, Mitzi Hannah, Joy-Lynn McCavit, Gwen Tucker, and Jon and Whitney Weddle for your patience, trust, and participation in being a part of my dream to equip the saints in hearing God's voice!

And to Linsey Wallace, Melody Botha, and Larry Sparks—favor is always found through relationships. I thank God you all came along and helped me or connected me to my next steps.

"In my experience, self-hatred is the dominant malaise crippling Christians and stifling their growth in the Holy Spirit."
—Brennan Manning

CONTENTS

INTRODUCTION

I had long forgotten who I was. Like everyone, experiences in life chipped away at what made me simply sacred—my union with God. It's a subtle sickness that eventually takes you over. Mostly a confident child, I grew to become utterly confused about my place in this world. Avoiding and hiding were tactical choices I made that only reinforced my proverbial weak spine. Why was I hiding? Who was I hiding from? Who was I? I was haunted by these questions—that is, until Holy Spirit showed up with better questions, questions that had the power to propel me somewhere new.

God knew me. He had never forgotten. So, He armed with me a pen, and I suddenly felt ten—no, twelve feet tall. Flattering me with questions, He showed me that my mind was creatively articulate and the light He created within me was brightly exposing—illuminating what had long been forgotten. He told me that as I wrote, my voice would grow stronger, wiser; God—such the exhorter.

He believed, so He spoke, and it was so.

I believe, so now I write; now I sow.

If you know me, you know I'm a narrative non-fiction junkie. I specifically like documentaries because through storytelling they reveal true events. So, naturally, in the middle of some night in 2013, I watched a Netflix documentary on pastors who gamble. Yes, I confess, I was fascinated by these literal holy rollers, so I tuned in with eyes and ears wide open. But it wasn't the dice throwing that these Bible-touting pastors held my attention with. It was a singular, inconsequential moment in the documentary when a young pastor, who influenced a congregation of hundreds, said that he'd never tell his parishioners that they could hear from God today. A hot heat rushed to my face.

Mostly a mellow gal, I was surprised by the way my body had a physical reaction to what was apparently a grieved heart. Big, hot tears fell from my eyes when I recognized, likely for the first time, the passion I carried for people knowing God through hearing His voice. I couldn't imagine where I would be without His presence, vision, and wisdom, which are all experienced prophetically.

Fueled by imaginings of thousands of people not knowing they could experience the most beautiful, gracious voice ever, I opened up my laptop and emailed my pastor at the time, Jay Bean, a short note to explain that I desired to begin teaching people how to hear from God. Surprisingly, I got a response minutes later with a *yes!* This is the work my hands have been set to since that night so many years ago!

Sometimes you'll discover what you're called to in the most practical of ways! Sometimes it's not lightning bolts or dreams of Jesus telling you what you're to be about when you discover the passions of your heart. Many times, when the advocate for the oppressed to be free is triggered within you, it reveals exactly what the work is that's been set before you. You may not have the answers for how to do it, but God will begin to give you vision and insight for it. I'm telling you, it's then that you discover real joy. Also, a little side note about passions—you'll know if you are passionate about something or if it's simply a hyped-up opinion that you have by the action you take. If it's passion fired up within you, you'll muster up the courage to do something about it. If it's just an opinion, you'll get over it within days and you'll carry on until the next thing you disagree with hypes you up. If God is the source of your passion, you'll find His favor waiting for you at the "Yes," along with an anointing of His grace to empower you far beyond your capabilities. If it's simply hyped disagreement that feels like passion, you'll have to use your own hot air to gain the momentum you desire, and that is exhausting.

Pastor Jay gave me a handful of weeks to begin working with people who desired to grow in hearing God's voice. I didn't know what I was doing. All I had going for me was that I trusted Holy Spirit would not leave a single person desiring to know God out in the cold. And I was right. Our group was full, and when word spread about it people who lived in other states asked if I could form an online classroom. Before long people from all over the country were awakening their own prophetic voices and growing in their personal relationships with God. Holy Spirit showed up in the most powerful, beautifully sincere ways.

Being a bridge for people to experience God didn't just start out of the blue because I watched a documentary. I had been leading people into hearing God for themselves within my day-to-day relationships up until that point, but I didn't recognize the need to actually begin formally equipping people until I acknowledged that there were people out there, like me, who had actually been equipped to shut down their God-given ability to hear God's voice. Injustice was staring me in the face, and the Holy Spirit was upon me to be an advocate and a helpmate for those who were experiencing God but had no one to talk to about it. Avoiding and hiding could no longer be the tactical route I used to retreat; instead, I was charged to take responsibility and action. I was awake, and suddenly I began to remember exactly who I was, who I always had been.

This is my story. I pray that hope will be sown into your heart, longings rekindled, and that you live in the wake of the revolution that afforded you an exuberant life.

Please proceed with the understanding that this book is not simply testimonies of my supernatural encounters with God; it's an invitation. Through the testimonies and teaching in this book, God will be inviting you to experience His mercy, love, and joy firsthand. Grab a pen, because at the end of this story I will provide you with devotional moments so that you can begin discovering your identity through knowing God and hearing His voice.

1

HOW MY PROPHETIC
LIFESTYLE BEGAN

I can tell you exactly the day when my so-called sacred faith took a screaming leap from the lofty pedestal it had been teetering on.

At the time, my husband was an ordained youth pastor who self-medicated with pornography. He was more than a little bitter, at times suicidal, and though he was an excellent provider his tendencies were to "stuff and puff." On the verge of an emotional breakdown, he stuffed his pain and then it came out in huff-and-puff rages that were emotional terror attacks. I, myself, was more of a "shove and unplug" type—a full-blown hidden stash of junk food in every room, an emotional binge eater who used food like a cutter uses a razor blade. Shoving food into my mouth and then unplugging from reality was my answer to coping with being the obligatory pastor's wife. I placated every emotion that made me uncomfortable, and those emotions always seeped their way out in the most destructive ways.

Ben and I were quite the pair back then, ten years ago, but it was my sincere belief that my marriage had been built on nothing more than devotion to a doctrine that hurt the most. I decided I was over all of it, any of it, whatever and everything "it" was. My 28-year-old heart, mind, and two-babies-later body was tired. Our seven-year marriage was over, according to me, as well as my belief in a God who seemed to be enjoying my torture. Spoiler alert: I'm still married to Ben and our babies are not so much babies anymore, but life back then was a nightmare.

"I'm done with you," I screamed into my hands. Withdrawn, attempting to disconnect from the person I felt was an all-consuming vacuum, never satisfied and continually vague, I groaned again, "I'm done with you, God."

Immediately after screaming at God, a deep mourning from within my soul came flooding to the surface. In the form of hot tears, my hands filled with emotions that I had been suppressing for years. All those moments when life terrorized my heart and I made excuses for it; all those moments handing my power over to a belief in something lifeless; all those moments trying to find intimacy in performance; all those moments—I sat there on the floor weeping and utterly exhausted. I had nothing left in me.

Then, interrupting my attempted divorce decree with God, an audible, otherworldly voice thundered from behind me, telling me to "Seek Holy Spirit." The presence I felt standing directly behind me was large and overshadowing. I couldn't turn to look. Frozen in the presence of something pure, I sat paralyzed in holy fear. With the words *seek Holy Spirit* vibrating within my bones, I was shaken. Unable to move my body, I simply sat in the presence of God. And as I sat there, encountering what I knew was truly

God's presence, a weighted air filled my room. The aroma gave off sweet impressions that something better, something more, was upon me. I dared not lift my head from my hands.

Eventually, I felt a lightness return to the air, beckoning me to stand to my feet. Wobbly, yet strengthened by a holy fear of God, I stood knowing I had just encountered sheer power that could have destroyed me, yet I was still alive and filled with so much hope for my future.

There is something really important about coming undone, letting everything go with no expectations for return. It was as if I had finally crawled out from hiding and stood before God, clothed in my shame, demanding He look at me. What I didn't understand at the time, but now see clearly as I look back on my life, was that God was not offended by my turmoil and conflict, my sin. He wasn't the cause of my angst either. In fact, I thought I was demanding He look at me, but He had been watching me all along, calling me out into the open. Calling a shamed humanity out of hiding is a God thing.

Your prophetic nature is simply your union with God revealing itself. When perfect love casts all fear out of your life, in that moment a prophetic lifestyle is born! This is why your soul, as well as every other part of you, is in the process of transforming into the image and likeness of God! Any desire to grow in the prophetic is a desire to know God and experience being known by Him.

When God sent a messenger to my bedroom commanding that I seek Holy Spirit, the weak, whittled idol of god that I had been worshiping paled in comparison to what I had just experienced. Holy fear of God is nothing other than remembering in reverence who your daddy is! It's the act of repentance, which means to take on God's perspective of what is true once again.

7

The moment Heaven erupted in my room, bowed in holy fear I knew the god I had been screaming at was not the God I was encountering. Holy Spirit is the one who convicted my heart with the remembrance of God's goodness, which led me to repentance—remembering that He is with me and He is good—and that was the beginning of awakening to my true identity. This was when all Heaven broke loose over my life and I began walking in what I call a prophetic lifestyle.

In the new covenant, Holy Spirit has been poured out on all of us (see Acts 2:17). Our union with God through Jesus has made knowing God, the ways of His Kingdom, and His heart toward the world as easy as remembering who God is! This is why we are *all* prophetic beings inside the new covenant!

Jesus said that He has restored within us a right spirit that cries Abba (Daddy God)! (See Romans 8:15.) We are children who know the perfect love of the Father! A love so perfect that it casts out all fear! A love so perfect that we, in turn, are commanded to love in the same way because in that love we share in likeness!

It's important that I walk us through this because the prophetic gift is not from God if it's not found within the context of the new covenant. The prophetic gift flows from the intimate relationship we have with God. The prophetic, in the new covenant, is purposed to honor the new command Jesus gave us—the law of love and forgiveness (see John 13:34). This one command sums up God's whole heart behind all spiritual gifts. If the prophetic gift in your life isn't empowering you to love or forgive the way God does, then I question not only the spirit you're operating in but I wonder what covenant you are abiding in.

The old covenant and the new covenant are not equal. The new covenant is even described in the Bible as a *better covenant* (see Heb. 8:6-7), and indeed it is! The old covenant revealed glimpses of God's nature but was focused on what man could do for God. The fruit of that covenant was nothing but broken people breaking promises over and over again. But through the old covenant God had a purpose! Galatians 3 explains that purpose was designed so God's people had a "guardian" that led them to Christ (see Gal. 3:23-26). Remember, God had rescued a people who had been enslaved for generations. Can you imagine what had been developed in them? His orphan-hearted, idol-worshiping people had a long way to go before they knew how to even operate within the context of a family. Meant as a tutor, the old covenant taught rules of how to function in a relationship, but it wasn't until Jesus came that we were able to see God's full heart for what being in a relationship with Him would look like.

Second Corinthians 3:14 says that the relationship God had with man within the context of the old covenant veiled Him:

> *But their minds were made dull, for to this day the same veil remains when the old covenant is read. It has not been removed, because only in Christ is it taken away.*

The Israelites, who had firsthand encounters with God's power and provision repeatedly and generationally, were veiled to the full picture of God that would only be found in Jesus.

Though God's nature was veiled as His orphaned children's hearts were being refined and readied for freedom in a relationship with Him, His intentions for His children were never hidden. After being delivered from slavery, in Exodus we read God speaking to His children's potential—a prophetic statement that echoed throughout the New Testament:

Now then, if you will indeed obey My voice and keep My covenant, then you shall be My own possession among all the peoples, for all the earth is Mine; and you shall be to Me a kingdom of priests and a holy nation (Exodus 19:5-6 NASB).

It has always been God's intention for us to be His and Him to be ours. We were always going to be an open-hearted people whose motives were pure and our remembrance of who God is would be accredited to us as righteousness. But that was never going to happen outside of Jesus, because God's hopes had never rested in man's ability; His hopes for humanity rested in Himself, His Son Jesus, and Holy Spirit! It's the work inside of this new and better covenant that brings about redemption through the revelation of who God is as our Father and who we are to Him as a child! With God it's always been and always will be about relationship.

Many times when we read the book of Genesis, specifically the part where Adam and Eve sin and hide from God, we forget that God, in that moment, related to mankind not just as a Creator interacting with His creation but as a Father would engage with His child. Adam was not just a toy that had gone defective and now God had lost interest. Long before Adam and Eve, before land kissed the sea, before the heavens shimmered and the earth rotated, God (the Father, Son, and Holy Spirit) imagined a family that would inherit a joy that surpassed all understanding. He dreamt of a people who would reveal His glory by walking in His likeness. Humanity was conceived in God's heart first, and it was in the imaginations of His heart that He decided He would take on the responsibility for this creation; He would be a Father. Fatherhood begins long before a baby is born. Fatherhood begins at the decision to take on the responsibility for one other than yourself.

Even on the other side of the Garden of Eden we find God fathering Adam and Eve's children—Cain and Abel.

> *Then the Lord said to Cain, "Why are you angry? Why is your face downcast? If you do what is right, will you not be accepted? But if you do not do what is right, sin is crouching at your door; it desires to have you, but you must rule over it"* (Genesis 4:6-7).

That conversation would have been a little different for today's parent. It would've sounded more like, "Fix your face! You can do better, I didn't raise a fool!" Obviously, God in all His wisdom says it so much better, but it's the same gist, right?

Parenting doesn't always go that smoothly, does it? I mean, even with God directly influencing Adam and Eve and Cain, they still seemed to get it wrong. But I don't believe God as a Father got it wrong! Even to Cain, who was cast out of God's presence after killing his brother (our sins may be forgiven, but our choices have consequences), God revealed His fatherly nature once again by marking him so that no enemies would attempt to kill him now that he would be going at life apart from God's direct influence (see Gen. 4:14-15).

I believe this is where we as believers make a very vital mistake. We forget that even in our sin, God is a Father to us first. Though we grieve His heart, He will not turn His back on His children. From the beginning, God walked with His children. They knew Him as their Father, not only their Creator. He has proven that over and over, but for us today our ultimate proof of

God relating to humanity from a Father's heart is found in the new covenant and looks like Jesus!

Jesus said if we have seen Him, we have seen the Father (see John 14:8-9). He is the complete picture of God, and it's not only through the lens of Jesus that we understand the Scriptures; we should be looking to Jesus for prophetic discernment, because the prophetic is God's perspective and voice. As Bill Johnson so famously says, "Jesus is the only perfect theology." To look upon Jesus is to know God fully! This also brings up another important point—when reading the Bible it's important to know which covenant with God people were operating in to understand the relationship between God and man in context. It's also important to make a distinction between the old and new covenant because how you understand and know God will become the filter that all prophetic experiences pass through. If you have any desire for the prophetic, then you seek to know God and experience being known by Him!

There are so many teachers, but not many fathers.

I feel like today we construct organizations and call them ministries before we've even served those in our immediate lives very well. We set up a social media page, file for nonprofit status, and go out field-of-dreaming it—*build it* and they come. It's true—build a shelter and the homeless will arrive with little effort. But I think when we skip the step of learning how to be fathered by God through Holy Spirit and don't turn and practice fathering/mothering within our daily relationships, the only thing that will really be built or offered to anyone is hierarchy—a pyramid scheme.

The reason Jesus came to reveal the Father was because the only way into the Kingdom was through a relationship within the context of family!

Being matured through the context of family first is necessary because having authority with no responsibility leads to tyranny. And having responsibility with no authority leads to slavery. Jesus dealt with these at the cross, but many reject it. Not all of us want or know how to be in a family. For those that reject it, we interact with the world around us as an orphan, as a victim.

In a family, the father and mother are consistently giving authority so the child can mature in responsibility. This equips a self-aware, powerful individual who knows how to manage himself as well as create an empowering atmosphere so others can do the same.

All I'm saying is, maybe we have this "ministry" thing backwards. Building organizations and calling them communities that have as much relational responsibility as a fast food cashier tends to create a lot of bitterness in a person who is timidly hoping to be a part of a powerful and loving community. Ultimately, as individuals it's our responsibility to grow in a relationship with Holy Spirit so that we can experience firsthand the family of God and then in turn be the family to those in our immediate lives.

LIVING FROM A FORGOTTEN IDENTITY

My husband and I, as I described in the beginning of this chapter, were the perfect example of living from a forgotten identity. Reared up by religion, shame became our tutor. But it was ineffective. All that shame developed in us was a no-good identity and a perceived disconnection from the only source that could tell us otherwise—God. Even more unfortunate, we had devoted our life to a doctrine that said God didn't speak to humanity presently because we were sinners. The effect of sin is shame, and shame always leads to hiding and a lifestyle cultivated by a forgotten identity. This is why God tells us that the wages of sin is death. When we stay hidden from the only source of complete acceptance, we never experience the perfect love that casts out fear and we stay hidden from the very one we were created in the image of—our Father God! This is death. There are many today who profess to be believers but their lives look more like a scene out of *The Walking Dead*.

Ben and I tried multiple times to find our own way out of hiding, but that only led to consistently falling short. We had compromised our own internal integrity so many times that we didn't even trust our own abilities to honor ourselves, let alone honor the vows we had made to one another. We were fully living from a forgotten identity, and it was destroying not only our marriage but us as individuals as well. We were losing ourselves to an unseen, unacknowledged battle with the very spirits that were coming against the knowledge of God and who we were to God.

Much like most of you reading this, the doctrine I was raised on taught me that I was depraved and God physically could not be in presence of sin; therefore, He was distanced from me. These doctrinal accusations about God's character made having a relationship with Him and knowing Him near impossible. And they are just that—accusations about God that come straight from the accuser himself, accusations that have been formed into doctrines of men.

Accusations against God's motives are how the enemy creates perceived separation. It's the tactic that was used on Adam and Eve, so of course it's the same old, tired tactic that is being used on us still today.

Check it out—Adam and Eve did not have a sin nature when they chose to disobey God in the Garden. There was nothing of or in them that was lacking or depraved. When they ate from tree of knowledge of good and evil, the only thing they gained was the knowledge of evil. They already had the knowledge of good.

I define evil as everything that comes against the knowledge of God, while sin is the result of agreeing with the accusations against God and how God has defined you—good! What humanity gained that day in the Garden of Eden was a mindset that was now open to the accusations that came against the knowledge of God and His goodness. This ultimately gave us a lens to view life apart from God, giving us the choice to live a life from a forgotten identity. If evil is the antithesis of good, and God called you good, then it is no wonder that one of the biggest assaults on God's creation would be against our likeness in God.

Called out of hiding, in Eve's response to God we find humanity's very first acknowledgement of a choice that was made from a forgotten identity. I love the way Young's Literal Translation translates her response:

> And Jehovah God saith to the woman, "What [is] this thou hast done?" and the woman saith, "The serpent hath **caused me to forget**—and I do eat" (Genesis 3:13 YLT).

What was it the serpent caused her to forget?

> Now the serpent was more crafty than any of the wild animals the Lord God had made. He said to the woman, "Did God really say, 'You must not eat from any tree in the garden'?"
>
> The woman said to the serpent, "We may eat fruit from the trees in the garden, but God did say, 'You must not eat fruit from the tree that is in the middle of the garden, and you must not touch it, or you will die.'"

"You will not certainly die," the serpent said to the woman. *"For God knows that when you eat from it your eyes will be opened, and you will be like God, knowing good and evil"* (Genesis 3:1-5).

Satan deceived Eve by telling her to focus on an apparent lack. He delivered his second blow by causing her to question God's motives and His intentions for her life, resulting in her forgetting what was true—she had all authority and dominion in the land God gave her; she lacked nothing and was made in the likeness and image of God.

Daily, the enemy is attempting to convince us to focus on perceived lack so that we should forget the promises we have in Jesus! Satan tempts us with fear of disappointment, which leads to our hopes being deferred. We then become heartsick and desperate, resulting in choices made from a place of forgotten identity.

Now Adam and Eve were experiencing shame for the first time. Sin will always, immediately, lead to shame because sin is an act that violates connection in our relationships. Shame is your soul's way of recognizing that love has been violated! The soul's signal that shame is present in your life—hiding yourself, withdrawing from community, shrinking back in conversations, a complete lack of self-control. All of us, because of sin, have experienced the effects of shame. Sadly, some identify so much with their sin and shame that they are unable to recognize the voice of God calling them out into the open. And believe me, He is calling, not because you're lost but because you're in fact found—you've just forgotten!

Psalm 34:5 says *"Those who look to him are radiant; their faces are never covered with shame."* When we remember God and who He is, we are wooed out of hiding and His grace removes our shame so that once again we can radiate His likeness to the world.

When I tell the story of how my journey to a prophetic lifestyle began, no one is much shocked that it started with Holy Spirit. After all, it is Holy Spirit who imparts all gifts. But I think what does shock people is that when I became awakened to my prophetic nature, it had nothing to do with a cool new supernatural function; rather, it had everything to do with me abiding in the remembrance that God perfectly loves me.

Being called out of hiding and being met with mercy instead of judgement, I felt the shame melt off of me and the fear disarmed. I stood in the presence of God and soaked in His satisfaction with me. Religion had taught me to identify more with Adam hiding in the bushes than I did with Jesus, the last Adam, who had been resurrected and seated in Heaven (see 1 Cor. 15:45). God had been waiting for me to throw the version of someone else's god away for a very long time—a process I am in daily. When the words "Seek Holy Spirit" illuminated all the dark corners of my heart, I experienced my first real breath as a born-again believer, even though I had been technically saved 20-something years prior. The hope I experienced was supernatural, and it still vibrates through my body when I recall that moment! Holy Spirit had always been with me, but now I was going to learn how to walk hand in hand in union with Him.

2

WAKING UP

What is that? I thought to myself.

The sermon started off like a thousand sermons before
it. There was a warm welcome to the congregation from Pastor Boomer and off he went preaching the gospel. I don't
recall much of what he said, but as he preached I noticed
what looked like a transparent, brightly glowing halo around
his head. I thought my eyes were just blurry. I rubbed my
eyes and took a second look—now his head and upper shoulders were completely glowing. What was I seeing? What was
happening? I looked around the room to see if anyone else
was seeing what I was seeing, and from their sleepy faces and
checked-out stares I could tell I was the only one. Maybe I
was hallucinating? I moved from the middle of the pew to
the end, thinking maybe it was the way the light was hitting
him, and when I did that the light intensified and grew larger,
finally engulfing his upper body completely.

Pastor Boomer stepped down of the stage, and his every movement was traced with a bright white light, streaming from his arms as he gestured when he spoke. Now it was undeniable—I was, in fact, seeing something quite bizarre. He had turned into what seemed to be a walking lightbulb, and it was freaking me out.

As I was watching this human glow stick preach, the first thought I had was that I would never ever be able to tell anyone about this. But the first thing I did was go to Heath, my older brother.

Hesitating with my words, I said, "Heath, today at church I saw…"

Interrupting my sentence, Heath said, "…the white glow? Did you see Pastor Boomer glowing?" he asked, and then quickly explained that he had been seeing it for years.

I was stunned and relieved that Heath could confirm that I wasn't having a stroke or, worse, simply losing my mind. But what were we seeing?

The next day I saw Pastor Boomer, and like an unfiltered toddler, I blurted out everything I saw as rapidly as I could. "Yesterday at church I saw your head glowing, and then your arms, and your shoulders too. And there were long streams of white light that came off your body as you spoke and moved. What is that?"

Pastor Boomer dropped his head and a tear rolled down his face. He looked back up at me, and in a kind of soft but short way he said, "That was Holy Spirit." I felt my entire body freeze up. He didn't know that I was on a personal mission from God to seek Holy Spirit—which at that time only consisted of reading every scripture that had the name Holy Spirit and quizzing everyone I ran into about who Holy Spirit was. Here I was, staring at a visibly touched pastor who was saying that I had just seen Holy Spirit. I was speechless, until I wasn't, and then I urged him to explain. He didn't explain though. Like a giant carrot dangling in front of my face—no, a piece of cake—I wanted more. He thanked me for my encouragement, though I didn't know I was encouraging him, and he changed the subject quickly.

It was strange—after that experience of seeing Holy Spirit empower Pastor Boomer as he preached the gospel, when I'd tell any leadership in the church about it, they'd all quickly change the subject. And in the most loving way possible they would tell me to stop seeking "that" out. Literally, I heard "stop seeking that out" almost a dozen times. That was frustrating. I wasn't seeking anything out, and it wasn't stopping either. After that day in that little Georgia church, I never saw the same way again. My eyes and ears were opened, my senses fully awakened. It was if a realm I always claimed to believe in—but if I'm being honest, I didn't believe in—was overlaid on top of my world! It was so overwhelming that I actually tried to be delivered from it by having someone pray it away. It was so shocking to my perceived reality that I begged God to make it stop and for me to go back to normal. What I didn't know at the time was this was normal Christianity. I was awake! I had been baptized by fire and all the scales on my eyes had been consumed by God's presence.

I never had anyone pray over me to be filled with Holy Spirit. I never asked for any gifts. All I did was seek after understanding, as God commanded, in the only way I knew how. It was that scan of the Scriptures, looking for every place with the name Holy Spirit, that revealed what I had devoted my entire life to, what I called my faith, was shallow and in vain. It is impossible to do a study on Holy Spirit, let alone study Jesus' life, and not question the so-called Christian lifestyle many of us are faithful to. I was challenged when I read about Peter's shadow healing sick people (see Acts 5:15-16), and I was uncomfortable when I read about angels unlocking prison doors (see Acts 5:19). I didn't feel too great when I read about the Day of Pentecost and Holy Spirit igniting the tongues of men (see Acts 2). The standard for what Jesus demonstrated as normal Christianity wasn't my normal, yet no one seemed to have a problem with that. And it's certainly likely that they didn't believe in it, that they embraced the doctrine of cessationism as I had. It was a convenient belief for those who embraced lack and lived from a forgotten identity. But here I was seeing angels and odd beings that looked like shadows and words written above people's heads with grotesque wounds appearing over people's bodies. I was hearing private prayers that people had been crying out to God. Angels were literally waking me up by bouncing the end of my bed so my feet would fall from the bed, alerting me that it was time to get up. I was smack dab in the middle of what felt like an alternate universe, and everyone around me was walking oblivious. I couldn't reconcile the doctrine that I had always clung to so tightly with what was happening, so I was left with the choice to abandon it, trusting Holy Spirit would lead me to the understanding I needed.

I had only confessed to my leadership about the glowing pastor from Georgia, and they told me to stop seeking that out. What would happen if I told them that I knew they were struggling with suicidal thoughts or that they were battling insecurities about their callings? Maybe they would've called me a witch or even worse a false prophet. But none of those worries plagued me in the beginning, because I felt alive and hopeful like I had never experienced before. That's a side effect of spending time with Jesus. With open eyes, I was beginning to see just how incredibly good God was, and though I didn't even know what the word *prophetic* meant back then I knew that God had opened my eyes, not just so I could see the unseen but so that I could co-labor with Him in doing something about it. Hope was abounding like never before.

I've come to understand, now that I embrace what is described as a naturally supernatural lifestyle, that the most supernatural thing that can ever happen to anyone is not seeing angels or seeing the sick recover—that just comes when you rest in your identity that is found in Christ. But the most supernatural thing has been the moments that God has allowed me to witness people hearing Holy Spirit's whisper that they are loved by God, leading them to call upon the name of Jesus as their King and find rest in who God says they are. I often run into religious folk who gently rebuke my belief that all people are prophetic and we can all hear God's voice, but all I need to remind them of is the time they called upon Jesus as their Savior. I ask them if they chose God first or if it was God who chose them first, and then they recognize that they have experienced the supernatural voice of God calling out to them at least one recognizable time in their life. And then I kindly suggest to them that if God spoke to them once, it may not be inconceivable that He might do it again, maybe even a lot.

There are a few reasons why I run into these rebukes. Obviously some are coming from a doctrinal standpoint, which I understand because that was my life, but a lot of the time, I believe, people do not believe they can hear God's voice because not only do they wrestle with identity issues and shame, but they also generally don't understand how they function as a triune being—a body with a spirit and soul—and they don't know how Holy Spirit communes with us. People generally reject things they do not understand, but in this case they are rejecting the very thing they were designed to do—walk with a God who is Spirit in the natural.

3

DESIGNED TO REIGN

When the prophetic really began to operate in my life, I was a senior at Missouri State University studying elementary education. I had only one semester left, student teaching, before I would graduate with my bachelor's degree. I would be the first out of my immediate family to graduate from college, and they were all very proud. On this specific day at a local elementary school, I was to be evaluated by my college professor in a fourth grade class where I was to teach a social studies lesson. Right before I took over the class, as I was waiting off to the side for the standing teacher to finish up her lesson, Holy Spirit washed down over me like a tidal wave. Unexpected, completely caught off guard, I quickly saw a series of visions of me doing different things—I was speaking with a group of women at a church somewhere; books were stacked up in front of me, implying I had written them all; and I saw myself traveling and encouraging and healing people. Voiced over that stream of consciousness about my future was the question, "What are you doing?" And it was asked in a literal type of way, a way that was encouraging me to speak out loud what Holy Spirit was revealing to me—an audible acknowledgement of what I was seeing. I didn't know it then, but it was definitely Holy Spirit teaching me how to declare and prophesy over myself.

The next thing I knew, the standing teacher was introducing me to the classroom, and I went on to teach my lesson—which I knocked out of the park, by the way. But after that school day, I sat in my car recalling the images that were still playing out over and over in my imagination. My heart ached because a depth of wonder and awe that I had not been in touch with before was calling, aching for me to agree with the promises that I felt impregnated by. That's when I decided, right then and there, that if there was even a remote chance that I was hearing right and I could actually spend my days connecting people to the Spirit of God, then that was something I was willing to believe in. I just needed to think about how I was going break it to my husband, who had been faithfully supporting me going back to school, who had been so looking forward to the future second income I was only one semester away from.

I felt a draw toward something bigger than me, and at the time I thought it was about the work. I thought that if I didn't do what I saw in those visions then I was going to mess up God's grand plans. I didn't understand that God was giving me an alternative choice, a choice that would require incredible faith but would develop me. I needed this—it would heal my soul in ways that I would have been too afraid to engage with on my own. My prosperity would be found as my soul was healed, and this was the journey that Holy Spirit was inviting me into. Walking with God has shown me that this life is about experiencing His salvation today, not trying to earn His pleasure. It is His great pleasure to invite you into impossibilities so you can experience what abundant living looks like.

Many of us want to hear what God has to say about our future, but we aren't willing to do anything with the vision outside of being entertained by it. Some of us are afraid of being disappointed, allowing our past to cast judgement on our potential. And some of us are only willing to embrace the dying process that all of our physical bodies are in because it's the only vision we've been repeatedly taught within the church—that we only prosper when we die and go to Heaven. Think about it—placing your hope in dying when Jesus said He came to give you life and life abundantly is contradicting to faith. He came so that you could advance His Kingdom, which is all about the revelation and gift of this supernaturally natural abundant life that's found in relationship with Him.

I believe God invited me to seek Holy Spirit so that I could not only experience knowing Him but experience what life in connection/relationship to Him looks like. It's pretty extravagant. I mean, have you read about Heaven? He paved His streets out of gold. Have you seen what Jesus did when He was on earth? They say there aren't enough books that can hold it all. Let's get real about what it means to share in God's glory! It's beautiful, it's loving and kind, but it's beyond your simple ability and it's wild! Your life is supposed to be bigger than what you by yourself could create. Your life is supposed to reflect what you and God in relationship can accomplish. This is why you're called a co-heir, an ambassador, a child of the living God! I believe to embrace a prophetic lifestyle is vital in truly advancing the Kingdom of God, which looks like God's children waking up and manifesting on earth their union with God, empowered by Holy Spirit. This life has never been about starting up ministries; its about learning how to truly live reconciled to God, which is the ministry of reconciliation that Christ has called us into!

As I began to become awakened to the potential of my new identity, Holy Spirit began to teach me to view myself in more of a holistic way versus a compartmentalized way. This brought tremendous balance to me as I learned how to honor the spiritual gifts on my life and understand Holy Spirit's role in reconciling me to God wholly, not just one part of me.

For me, early on, that looked like seeing and hearing the promises Holy Spirit revealed to me and then allowing that prophetic hope to heal the part of my soul that was shut off and shut down from going after more. For example, in the story I just told you about Holy Spirit falling on me in the classroom, holistically walking this out looked like me physically going to my husband and telling him that I'm believing in me as much as God does, which meant dropping out of college so that I could learn how to possess the promises God had placed on my life. It started out with believing in something unseen and then practically walking it out in the little ways I was able to at the time—writing down my testimonies and my experiences and teaching those closest to me how to possess the promises God was speaking over their own lives. Nothing glamorous there, but very supernaturally natural and incredibly powerful.

With each testimony written and each choice I made that agreed with the promises God had shown me over my life, I was reintroduced to the familiar woman in me who had been waiting to be recognized by no one other than myself. I liked her. A lot. She was radiant as her face was set upon the Lord! I found a lot of favor when I began to practically walk out the spiritual things God was showing me as well. For example, five years later Missouri State contacted me by letter to tell me that I had actually earned my bachelor's degree if I wanted to simply reapply to MSU (for free) and apply to graduate! I received my bachelor's degree in general studies with an emphasis in business in the mail several months later. Come on! How faithful is God! Talk about redemption! I had always felt embarrassed to tell people that I dropped out of college with only one semester left because I believed God was offering me a better gig.

I'd like to make a distinction here. When I say better, I am not saying holier. For me it would be a better gig because it was awakening me to the potential in me that I had stopped believing in. The teaching profession is a sacred profession. God is faithful to complete what He starts, even if doesn't look like we are. And He always rewards those who walk by faith! This is salvation working through each part of us. Faith is walking out that salvation in fear and trembling, in holy remembrance of who God is and who you are to God! Believe me, the trembling part is real, but remember, to know God is to know He can be trusted!

First Thessalonians 5:23-24 says: *"May God himself, the God of peace, sanctify you through and through. May your whole spirit, soul and body be kept blameless at the coming of our Lord Jesus Christ. The one who calls you is faithful, and he will do it."* Paul clearly distinguishes three parts that make us up—spirit, soul, and body. He also said it is God Himself who sanctifies you and keeps you holy. This is the work of Holy Spirit!

Most believers are comfortable with the idea that when we die, our natural body will go back into the dirt and the non-physical part of us will go to Heaven in the twinkling of eye, as is our promise as a believer (see 1 Cor. 15:52), but maybe not all of us exactly understand the three parts of us that Holy Spirit is renewing and sanctifying. Maybe we aren't exactly sure what functioning as a whole looks like. And some may not understand that we don't have to wait until we die and get to Heaven before we begin walking in our new creation that is found in Jesus, because Jesus died and rose again to get Heaven inside of you today! Today is the day that Lord has made! Today is the day that every circumstance, everything can change when you begin to see yourself found in Christ—not lacking, not orphaned but found and wholly loved!

Hebrews 4:12 says that *"the word of God is alive and active. Sharper than any double-edged sword, it penetrates even to dividing soul and spirit, joints and marrow; it judges the thoughts and attitudes of the heart."*

Though you are one being, each part of you—spirit, soul, and body—is being actively brought into wholeness and purity by the Word of God, which the Bible clearly describes all throughout as being Jesus Christ. The spirit of prophecy, which is the spirit of Jesus, is the Word, and it says that the Word became flesh. Holy Spirit is speaking the Word of Christ over us, and it's a prophetic lifestyle and believing in the Word of God that actively brings us into wholeness. When we believe in Jesus and place our faith in His Word over our life, we can walk in truth as the person God says we are and live an abundant life!

One of Holy Spirit's beautiful pursuits is to reveal to you who Jesus is and what He has done for you. It's by grace, God's unearned love, and by His supernatural power and truth that you are actively being transformed in your spirit and soul, which then manifests through your physical body. I have heard multiple testimonies of people receiving God's abundant love only to find they have been healed from a sickness or depression has left them. This is the beauty of Jesus' gift of salvation at work! When we place our faith in the spoken Word of God over our lives, it is not just so one part of us can be reconciled to God; it impacts us body, soul, and spirit and reconciles us wholly to God!

The word *salvation* in Greek is *sozo*. It means to save, heal, recover, deliver, protect, preserve, to do well, and to be made whole—your entire human being (Strong's #G4982).

Jesus came not only so that we could have eternal reconciliation with Abba but so that we would walk in supernatural and natural wholeness with God on earth in our whole being! Placing our faith in Jesus' accomplishments alone grants us Heaven's success on earth. We become victors, as Christ is victor! God's love is not just for one part of us; it's for our whole being. We are new and whole in Christ, and we have been given eternal life with God, as mentioned in John 3:16.

Eternal life in Greek is *aionies zoe*. It refers to the miraculous perpetual life you simply receive upon believing—we can't earn it, we receive it (Strong's #G166).

Sozo is the whole package, and it comes by faith and trusting in the Word of God, Jesus, who is sanctifying us. When it's said that we are to work out our salvation with fear and trembling, I take this to mean that you honor the Word of God in your life above all else—so much that it produces action! It's not about striving to earn something from God. Your belief animates your life! What you see is what you become! Jesus told the woman in Luke 8:48 to go in peace; Jesus told the man at the pool at Bethesda to pick up his mat and go (see John 5). Just like those who placed their faith in the spoken word of God, which is Jesus, and received His grace and truth, we are forever changed; they believed, received, got up and went! When we receive the gift of eternal life (aionies zoe), a life of wholeness (sozo) is ours to walk out by keeping our eyes on what He has done!

Your new identity that is found in Christ activates with the spoken word of God! What is it God is speaking over you? What are the promises that He has uniquely given you? Have you seen yourself through His eyes? Have you heard all that He has planned for you? This is why living a prophetic lifestyle is so important.

4

NOT EVEN THE DOGS WILL BARK

Faith in Holy Spirit perfecting me was not just fun when I was awakened to God's voice, it became joy unspeakable. Jesus' yoke truly is easy and His burden is so, so light. I felt like the earth, in all of her imperfections, was a gift God had given me, and I had real power to impact it.

When we receive God's empowering grace, our faith grows and we begin to take on our sphere of influences with power. Grace doesn't empower you to be lazy; it calls you to rise up and become a change agent! Praise God that Jesus gave us back the authority to have dominion over the earth! When you truly know God and walk with Him, the world becomes your oyster! Obviously, we have opposition and tension, but those become opportunities to walk in your identity at a greater level, increasing your faith in God at new depths!

Because of Jesus, we are an entirely new creation. Placed on this giant Garden of Eden that we call earth, we don't hide when we hear the voice of God calling out to us as Adam and

Eve once did. When we feel the vibrations of His footsteps coming in pursuit of us, we recognize that this is the process of Him making all things new! Whatever impossible circumstance we face as God's children will indeed bow its knee to King Jesus! It's being back in God's presence, hearing the word that He is speaking over your life when everything has the hope of becoming new!

I remember when Holy Spirit began demonstrating what I was learning about impacting my spheres of influence naturally and supernaturally.

It was around 7 A.M. on a crispy fall morning, and I was awakened by an angel bouncing the end of my bed. As soon as I opened my eyes, I heard Holy Spirit say, "Let's go for a run." I don't run, first of all. I'm not an exercise person. I don't really trust people who are. (That's a joke.) But, the suggestion to spend time with God while running certainly made me question if I heard correctly. Maybe that was actually the devil trying to give me a heart attack. No, I kid, I knew it was God, and I argued with Him—but He nudged me out the door.

As I began to warm up with a quick-paced walk, He made mention of the dogs that I'd be passing on this familiar one-mile loop. There were about four or five dogs on this routine walk that gave me a momentary scare even though I knew they were there because they'd pop out and ferociously bark at me through the fence as I walked past their yard.

Holy Spirit told me to point my finger at the dog and say out loud "hush" and the dog would be silenced. I giggled out loud. At this point I was starting to think that I was making all of this up. First running and now silencing unruly dogs with a point of a finger. But I was entertained and thought, *Let's test this out.* I rounded the first corner and knew a dog was waiting in the upcoming yard. As I approached the fence, per usual, he rushed the fence and began his gnarly bark. As ordered, I pointed my finger and whispered "hush." I mean, only I'm allowed to think I'm crazy. I didn't want to give anyone who may be watching evidence that I'm loony toons by commanding a neighbor's dog to hush. To my surprise, the whisper and weak pointing silenced the dog. As if on cue, when the words rolled off my tongue the dog sat right down on his bottom and watched me pass by in silence. I laughed and thought that maybe he was a well-trained dog that silenced and sat on command.

As I approached the next house, the dog, like the first, rushed the fence and began barking. I wasn't quite to his yard yet, but I thought if this is God then proximity shouldn't matter, and I pointed my finger and said hush—again in a whisper. The dog instantly silenced and sat. I started laughing. I got closer, then right in front of him, and then walked right past him and he watched me clumsily jog by. Could this really be God? If so, why is this happening? I didn't really understand, but it made me laugh. I got to the next house and the dog ran up to the fence, but this time as I approached, before I could do the whole point and hush thing, he laid down and didn't move a muscle as I ran by. I couldn't believe what was happening. I had walked this mile loop almost daily and these dogs were always obnoxiously protecting their backyard patch. Miracles were happening, and it wasn't just because I was actually moving my body faster than a walk. I finished my jog and not one dog barked as I got near them.

When I got home, I plopped myself down on the couch and asked Holy Spirit what that was all about. I heard *Exodus 11:7.* So I picked my tired body off the couch and hobbled over to my son's New Living Translation Bible that was sitting on the table.

As soon as I read it, I sat down at my kitchen table and began to worship God!

> *But among the Israelites it will be so peaceful that not even a dog will bark. Then you will know that the Lord makes a distinction between the Egyptians and the Israelites* (Exodus 11:7 NLT).

This moment, as silly as it seemed, became an anchor point in my life. I began to see clearly that God was defining me as His own, and as His very own I would walk with an authority simply by being marked as His.

Walking with God still requires walking. There is an effort on our part that is required, but He has marked us as His own, and anywhere we go the enemy will cower in acknowledgment of who our Father is! The only question is, do you know it? The world will see it and call it many things, but do you see it and know that you've been anointed with authority and given a voice to powerfully live your life and impact the lives around you?

This brings me to an important point in not only awakening your prophetic voice but in learning to abide in your prophetic nature. You've been chosen first! This is no small revelation. God wants you to experience what it's like to walk with Him unhindered. He wants you to learn to walk with Him knowing you've been marked and made new. His love for you is not because of what you can do for Him but because of who He is. You are not God's ultimate project. You've never been a project. You've been His child. He's not wringing His hands hoping you'll behave correctly. I sincerely believe that God wants you to experience being known by Him through personal prophetic encounters with Him. He wants you to experience knowing and being known. It's a powerful posture that Jesus has put you in—to see and know God, abiding in perfect love and learning to reign from Heaven.

5

PROSPEROUS SOUL

My spirit was alive and active. A part of me that had been dead was now resurrected by Holy Spirit. He revealed God as a good Father and what it was like to have Jesus as my King. I began to see what it was like to function in the Kingdom of Heaven while being present on earth. It was exhilarating. I felt alive, not because I was awakening to all these spiritual realities but because I finally felt like I was home and Holy Spirit was establishing me in that home. That didn't mean that all of the life that I had lived didn't have consequences on my soul. My emotions, my will, and my mind needed to be touched by God as well.

If there is anything that I've experienced about God it's that He is a creative genius. He doesn't only know how to use the eraser; He is very good at taking something old and creating something entirely new out of it. He knows full well that every little ding and dent in the clay is just an opportunity to smooth something entirely new into the creation's functionality and personality. Ultimately, we are fashioned to be overcomers. Rooted in victory, our only outcome is to thrive! Right now, in this very moment, all of us have an opportunity sitting before us. We all have something in our life, some life area that needs overcoming—that needs Holy Spirit to cast a vision so we can see how to walk through it victoriously in wisdom and in power. It's going to require not only spiritual wisdom, but it will also require your heart to be open to whatever it needs so that you can occupy the victory that Christ has made way in advance for you.

I think for a long time I thought walking with God was about accomplishing something, and that's the thing about embracing a prophetic lifestyle. You get glimpses of your future, of the things you and God can do together, and you think it's about doing those things, but that's not it. God's not showing you a task list; He's giving you glimpses of what you look like in union with Him. He's not giving you images of how you will be behaving if you want to please Him. He's showing you how pleased He is with you and what you can do if you rest in that wealthy place of God's pleasure. Holy Spirit is in the great work of healing your heart so that when you begin to see Heaven on earth you will create; it's from a place of being, not doing. It's from a place of joy, not striving.

God's perfect love is in the process of casting out everything that opposes our reality found in Christ. What remains once fear is gone? Vision of a life that is overcoming anything that doesn't align with Heaven's best for our lives.

God has used angels, prophetic visions, words of knowledge and wisdom so that I would know Him and others would experience being known by Him. It's been inside of this love connection that Holy Spirit has been maturing me. It's been a long road of mistakes—embarrassing ones at that—which have shown me that it's never been about maturing in the gifts; it's about Holy Spirit using the gifts to mature me in His infinite love. It's through the gifts that I've learned how I can only honor this natural body and world that He's placed me in by embracing the supernatural. I've not just been learning how spiritual gifts work; I've been learning how He, God, moves and thinks and operates. Though He is mysterious in His ways at times, it's no mystery that I'm called to know and be known by Him (Father, Son, and Holy Spirit).

Once I began to have prophetic experiences with God, I started to understand these experiences like currency. God was putting money in my spiritual bank account so that I could spend Heaven on earth. These encounters had tangible, practical applications that were leading me into incredible things that I never thought were possible for my life. I used my journal like a bank account. Everything that began to happen to me—every time I even wondered if God was speaking to me, highlighting some thing or person to me—I journaled it down. I was becoming a wealthy woman, so to speak, and it gave me a boldness to approach people, to step into things that I felt fear in doing but did anyway because I knew God was with me. Journaling down every experience, every encounter helped me discern what God was revealing to me about Himself, and it was healing my soul. The areas of life where I felt abandoned and not protected were not consuming my thoughts as much. I felt freer and lighter because I was learning how to possess this spiritual currency— the prophetic—and spend it, resulting in favor in my life. Simply put, I was, for the first time, walking in belief, and my faith for the impossible became my normal.

In my studies during college, I remember watching a teaching by Rick Lavoie. It was called "When the Chips Are Down." He asked the audience to think of a child's self-esteem like poker chips. Each child has a number of poker chips that is increased by good things happening to the child or decreased when bad things happen. Whether they want to play in the game or not is moot; everyone has to play in this game called life. Rick challenged the audience by asking them what they thought happened when a child who has a low number of chips (self-esteem) is asked to play with a kid who has an endless number of chips; how would he play the game? There are two likely outcomes for the child with few poker chips.

1. The child who has the lower self-esteem can't afford to take necessary risks because of fear of losing what little he has, so he clings to it, guards it, defends it, and ultimately never gains. All he does is focus on the little he has; he never takes risks to grow his potential and never gains more chips out of fear of loss and disappointment.

2. The child who has the lower self-esteem hopelessly, recklessly throws it all away. He goes all in with no wisdom or self-control. Lack of vision of the potential he's holding will ultimately lead him to losing it all, quickly.

Whether we like it or not, we are a part of this game called life. Some of us wake up every day crying out to God that we don't want to play, that we don't have enough chips to play in the game. We've played the part of the beggar and the pleader, seeking out those we think may throw a few more chips our way—not that we'd know how to play any better even if we had more of a fair playing ground.

I'm not saying it's going to be easy. I'm not saying things will always be fair. I am saying that you've been prophetically empowered to change the game instead of being a victim of the game. You may have been playing by rules that God never gave you. Matthew 6:33 says it better than me: "Seek first his kingdom and his righteousness, and all these things will be given to you as well." The Kingdom is your origin point. You are seated with Christ in heavenly places. His righteousness is your perspective. Focus on the things above, and God will show you how to become the expert player in your own life!

Some of you are being called into the impossible things. Honestly, it's all of us, but some of you are actually awakened to it. God is with you. He will provide what you need, but you will have to learn how to navigate the conflict of your soul pulling you back into the past and the hope of glory calling you into the future. You cannot avoid the tension that comes with walking with God; you simply learn how to walk with and like Him. We do this by spending time in His presence. In His presence you will begin to see and hear things, and from that place a prophetic language is developed within you—this is the language that moves mountains.

For me it looked like this—my husband found me still in my towel from my morning shower, ten hours after he had left me earlier that morning. It was now early evening and I hadn't moved. Not one inch. I was panicked on the inside, but on the outside I couldn't force one tear. My emotions and my body were not in unity. It felt like I was going to die in this skin shell, but I wanted to live first. Where was the God who was whispering me jokes so that I could have a laugh when life seemed to be a little too serious? I needed a joke. I needed Him. I had been crying out to Him for over a month, but nothing—nada, crickets—and the silence had finally caught up to me.

By the way, sometimes God's so-called silence is His way of working out some really bad theology (beliefs about who He is). It's not Him withdrawing love or affection or changing His mind about who you are; it's Him not agreeing with what you're attempting to pin on Him. I'm just being transparent here, and we've all done this. We believe we heard from on high and then blame a bunch of stuff on God that in reality we either incorrectly interpreted or placed too many of our own expectations on the word while simultaneously releasing all responsibility of working out the word by "waiting on God." God is not sending sickness to teach you lessons. He's not trying to torment you so you can relate to His Son's experience. Life is real and each choice has consequences, good or bad. God will send angelic intervention to help you overcome these choices, but ultimately God is maturing His Bride into a people who don't avoid discipline and don't shy away from hard things but with a sound mind can make choices from a place of power and love.

Ben found me in crisis. From the beginning of my seeking out Holy Spirit, I would say the supernatural, at this point in my journey, had become my normal, and that seemed to be easing up as soon as I began to do the things I had seen in the vision I had in the classroom that day. It wasn't just a lack of feeling God's presence that I was experiencing—it was not seeing the angelic or getting prophetic insight for the people around me. I felt spiritually dry and thirsty.

I grasped for scriptures that had been stored in my heart, hoping for them to illuminate my path out of this pit, but they were tainted with a doubting voice that had a sarcastic spin. And you know that cheesy saying, "My prayers were hitting the ceiling"? I had never experienced that before, but this dark cloud hanging over me was doing just that, absorbing my words and raining them back down over me, mocking me. My hope had been stolen. My heart had grown sick.

I saw for myself how good God was and heard the plans He had for me; my journal was overflowing with spiritual currency, so to speak. The problem was I didn't know how to steward these words outside of supernatural encounters and experiencing His tangible presence. When it all stopped, I took it to mean God stopped moving. So I stopped moving and then I felt abandoned, but it wasn't actually that clear going through it. I started doing what a lot of us do outside of big encounters and angelic visitations—I began to over-complicate and hyper-spiritualize everything.

Before I knew it, the prophetic words I received from God were being eroded with doubt. What was just months ago so simple and clear for me was now in question! What if all the things I was seeing and hearing were delusions of grandeur? What if I was delusional, or worse yet had some type of mental illness? What if I mess up the wonderful things God has for me by making a wrong choice? Did I do something wrong?

I didn't move unless I felt a twinge of Holy Spirit. This meant I didn't write unless I felt a spiritual inclination for me to write. I put the pen down if I felt that spiritual presence leave. I began to develop superstitious rituals that I thought would please God enough to bring Him back so that I could continue to work on the vision He had given me. It all felt so holy. It was actually my own religion that I had developed and didn't know it. God now seemed imbalanced to me. It wasn't God. It was me. In the craze of my doing, I never stopped to reflect that this was not at all how God was when I was physically encountering His presence, so I was unable to recognize that in all of my doing I had stopped being. I was performing.

This is where I feel a lot of people are—stuck in the "I only do what God tells me to and when God tells me to do it." This is not a sound mindset and is not from God. If you're doing that, stop it! It led me to reverting back to the person who never really knew God in the first place. I began to doubt if God would really come through, and I began to mentally break down. I would release all my responsibilities and "wait on God," dismissing that God is always in the business of empowering me to exercise self-control (self-control means to control one's self) from the place of wholeness in Him. I spiraled into an extreme depression that went on for months. When Ben came home that day, I was at my rock bottom!

I heard Ben walk down the hallway and enter our bedroom. In a paralyzed state, I never budged. I don't know if I am a good enough writer to explain to you what it is like to experience hopelessness, though I truly believe people, even believers, are living in varying degrees of it daily. Some of you reading this now are probably connecting and know exactly what I am talking about.

So here I was, lying on my bed with my husband standing over me. In silence he stood staring, but his face was screaming his heartbreak. He eventually sat down on the bed beside me and put his hand on my shoulder. Ben's touch signaled to my heart that everything was okay, I had just forgotten. Ben's presence brought me a sense of peace—that is, until I heard Holy Spirit say to me in that moment, "Ben, has a word for you." My peace was replaced with anxiety because I knew Ben, at that time, struggled with the idea that God was involved with humanity intimately. He trusted what I had been experiencing was real because he knew me, but I think he believed God reserved those kinds of experiences for only certain people (this is not true, by the way).

I looked at him and told him that God had given him something to share with me. Wide-eyed, he stuttered, "What? No. I don't have anything. What...?" and then he blurted out, "Rosh Hashanah."

Perfect, I thought to myself. *I need English right now, not Hebrew.* "I don't know what that means, Ben."

He began to describe to me how Rosh Hashanah was the celebration of the new year. Information came rolling out of his mouth as if he had written an encyclopedia article on it. God was giving him insight into this Jewish holiday. And as he began to prophesy over me that it was a new year, it was a new season for me, his eyes widened and they filled with tears. He wasn't looking at me anymore, but he was seeing something within me. I sat up on the bed because I could visibly tell that something was happening with Ben.

"Ben? Are you okay?" He sat there staring at me and then began to reach his hand toward my face. I scooted away from him a bit to try and make sense of what was happening.

"Betsy, you have a veil covering your face, and Holy Spirit is telling me to lift the veil."

"What?" I saw nothing but understood that Ben was encountering God in a very powerful way and seeing spiritually. Tears streamed down his face. As he reached out toward me, he motioned as if he was lifting a veil away from my face—then he began crying and laughing. He put his hands over his mouth and whispered in awe through his hands, "Betsy, you are so beautiful. Oh, Betsy, you are so beautiful! You face is shining so brightly and your hair looks as if it is made out of pure gold."

As soon as the words left his mouth, a memory came flooding back to me of me when I was four or five years old. I had gotten out of my bed to go to the bathroom to get a drink of water. In our bathroom, my mom had placed a little stool by the sink, and I would go in there and put my mouth under the faucet to catch a drink. This particular night, I walked into the bathroom and got a drink of water, but when I stood upright while shutting off the water, my reflection in the mirror was outshining the bathroom lights and beamed back at me. My face was radiating a bright white light and my hair looked like long strands of gold. The only way I could describe that moment was that I knew God and I knew that I was His child. The moment impacted me so much that I remember thinking my dirty blonde hair was actually made of pure gold. That moment made such an impression on my little heart that I actually believed my hair was made out of gold for several years.

Now Ben and I were both standing to our feet. Ben began to declare over me that I was a new creation, in a new season, that this was a holy new year for me, and I was about to enter into a life I had never experienced before with God. Talk about power! That familiar presence of what felt like holy fire covered my body. That was the day that my marriage permanently changed. Remember what I said earlier about God using the prophetic to reconcile us wholly unto Him (spirit, soul, and body)? It applies not only to an individual but to the relationships you have with others as well! This very power that reconciles relationships is the same power that God used to change the world through Jesus. Supernatural reconciliation, demonstrated by Jesus and empowered by Holy Spirit in our everyday relationships, is the only true calling we have. My husband saw me in a brand-new light after that night. Once you get a glimpse of someone the way God sees them, it's impossible to see them in any other light. Once you know how they are known to God, any behavior that contradicts the truth of who they are is easy to recognize, making it easy to not judge them but love them by reminding them of who it is they've forgotten they are. This is amazing grace in action! This is how God's perfect love casts out fear and covers a multitude of sins!

God revealed to Ben my origin story with Him—a story that life had stolen away. God was not only exposing me to Ben in the light of His glory—a supernatural act that unified us as a couple in a way that therapy and counseling never could accomplish—but He was reminding me that I needed to go back to the beginning, back to my beginning with God. Back to when He chose me long before I ever began to strive for His attention or believe I had to perform for His affections.

He chose me first, and that wasn't changing. What was so brilliant about this well-timed move of God was that after that experience as a little girl in my bathroom, I specifically remember telling my mother the next morning that my hair was actually made of pure gold and about my encounter with God. I had a witness! So, after Ben reminded me of my origin story with God, I called up my mom and asked her about "the girl with the golden hair." Not only did she remember it, but she remembered me actively engaging angels and talking to God from the time I was very young. The innocence and ease of my relationship with my Maker came rushing back to me as she recalled stories of observing me as a child. We cried and laughed together on the phone because she too remembered experiencing very similar moments with God and angels when she was very young. Recalling the stories of your relationship with God always brings us right into worship—your weapon against anxiety and depression.

You've got to start seeing yourself the way God sees you—free, empowered with self-control, and incredibly wealthy with His wisdom and ways. It's important that we remain in that truth regardless of encounters and supernatural happenings. The truth is God is present whether you feel it or not. This is our reality as partakers in this new covenant. A huge part of learning to walk with God in spirit is learning how to walk with Him in truth. The truth is you've been anointed to hear God's voice and to abide in His presence. In Exodus 33:14-17, Moses was right to say to God that he would not go without God's physical presence, for how else would he know if he had favor with God? However, we are in a different covenant with God. We are in a covenant in which His presence has been poured out! It's beyond our feeling, our seeing, and our doing; it's simply our reality. A big reason I fell into such a depression was because as Holy Spirit was awakening me I began to encounter God's tangible presence nonstop. The things that were unseen I could see. The supernatural unfolded all around me, and as soon as that seemed to ease up I was too afraid to move. I thought God was gone. So I panicked and begged and all over again forgot. Jesus revealed a different picture of walking with God than Moses did.

Luke 4:1-2 says, *"Jesus, full of the Holy Spirit, left the Jordan and was led by the Spirit into the wilderness, where for forty days he was tempted by the devil. He ate nothing during those days, and at the end of them he was hungry."*

Jesus wasn't externally looking for signs and wonders filled with Holy Spirit; He became the sign and wonder. It doesn't say that Holy Spirit left Jesus when He entered the wilderness; it says that Jesus was full of Holy Spirit! Instead of looking externally for signs of favor, Jesus demonstrated what it looks like to grow in favor with God. Yes, Jesus grew up in favor with God and with man (see Luke 2:52). Jesus didn't run about seeking prophetic affirmation from those around him. He lifted His eyes to His Father and in that place was affirmed. When Jesus was being tempted by the devil, He battled from His posture of knowing and being known. When the devil tested whether He knew who He was, Jesus was found knowing.

My point in saying all this is—we must be awakened to the truth that God's spirit is dwelling within us. Jesus made sure of that! We can now walk in a confidence and a peace that surpasses our own understanding because Holy Spirit is renewing our mind constantly to His understanding. You won't always have a supernatural encounter or experience to affirm the favor that is already on your life, and that's by design. I'm not saying that His external presence ceases and we don't have any more tangible experiences of God's presence and it just becomes a knowing thing. I'm saying at some point God wants your faith to be rooted in Him. He does not want you drawing your identity from spiritual gifting or only supernatural abilities. Those are good and need to be honored, but your identity is found knowing you are His and He is yours. Luke 10:19-21 says it better than I:

> *"I have given you authority to trample on snakes and scorpions and to overcome all the power of the enemy; nothing will harm you. However, do not rejoice that the spirits submit to you, but rejoice that your names are written in heaven." At that time Jesus, full of joy through the Holy Spirit, said, "I praise you, Father, Lord of heaven and earth, because you have hidden these things from the wise and learned, and revealed them to little children. Yes, Father, for this is what you were pleased to do."*

Because you are filled with Holy Spirit, you will become a sign and wonder, revealing who your Father is—revealing the glory that has been placed on you. But if all of those encounters and all the signs and all the wonders ceased (they won't), you will be found full of joy because at the end of the day it's always been about you being God's child. It's as simple as that.

After Ben encountered how I was known to God and he reminded me of my origin story with God, I began the journey of learning how to lay down the chase of Holy Spirit and simply be indwelled by Him. It was no longer my feelings indicating if God was present; it was me acknowledging that He always was, always has been, and always will be beyond anything I felt. I could feel my proverbial spine strengthening and a boldness to take on my life living with God's eternal Yes and Amen over my life, trusting I'd be able to recognize the voice of God if plans changed.

Holy Spirit is giving you glimpses of incredible things, and with an awakened prophetic voice you will look at the impossibilities, at your limitations—and believe me, you have limitations—and you will say aloud, "Not today, you impossible thing! Stand aside!" The mountain certainly doesn't know it yet, but it's moving with each step you take toward it. Why? Because you've been called to overcome the very thing that's blocking your view, that's obstructing your path. Because you are filled with Holy Spirit. God's justice won't be had when we allow impossibilities to dictate what's true instead of us proclaiming what's true to the impossibilities!

God is balancing the scales of justice in this hour, but it's inside of impossibilities. Your soul is longing for the impossible. Your soul is aching for something new! It's the cry of the new creation within you that's longing to be acknowledged and lived out. But you will have to declare for it to rise up!

Proverbs 13:4 says: *"The soul of the sluggard craves and gets nothing, but the soul of the diligent is made fat"* (NASB).

Essentially, this is saying your soul is going to crave, it's going to desire, but if you're not managing it you'll reap nothing. You are a being who was created with emotions. You were created to allow those emotions to give you information, not dictate what's true. Not acknowledging your emotions only leads to you being managed by them, and allowing your emotions to be the captain of your ship leads to constant offense and being misinformed.

The health of your soul is vital to you walking in victory or walking like a victim. Holy Spirit is indwelling us so that our soul sings out *it is well!* When our spirit, soul, and body are in alignment, everything around us experiences God's justice because what remains is His righteousness.

You were designed to hope, to have dreams, and to desire more. But someone whose hopes have been deferred because their soul is ignored and unmanaged will not only find themselves heartsick—depressed and anxious—they will embrace the dying process and check out of this gift that is life. Hope deferred may make you heartsick, but longings fulfilled—hopes of the heart (your soul)—are a tree of life!

Your soul was designed to inform you of the happenings of your heart. It's your diagnostic center that something needs to be managed. Of course, it doesn't have the final say in the matter, but it's the alert that something within your heart needs to be looked at and filtered through the mind of Christ. As we take on the mind of Christ, we not only become powerful and manage our hearts in a controlled manner filtered through wisdom, we begin to reap the fruit that's being grown on this tree of life that we are taking from. Our soul grows fat and our heart is happy because we begin to self-manage and partner with God in this thing called life!

Don't take it from me; take it from God—you were created to have a fat and happy soul! But that's because you're over-coming—you're walking through hard things, having the hard conversations in order to bring healing to your relationships and not ignoring or avoiding life. You're seeing obstacles and think-ing opportunities. You are empowered because instead of just seeing things naturally, you see things spiritually. You no lon-ger partner with performance and no longer believe the lie that you can mess this up. You're getting all kinds of intel now from your whole being as well as Holy Spirit. You're checking in on your emotions, on your gut instincts, reminding yourself what it is that God has said to you and about you. You even ask for new vision, and then you use self-control. You self-manage and you make choices like a free person would—powerfully informed, richly able to take the risk.

This is where awakening your own prophetic voice and nature is vital! I've noticed once people begin to walk and talk with God, they get prophetic visions and words about their potential and purpose; they go through a struggle very similar to what I went through. The prophetic taps into the eternity that is housed within us. It taps into the bigness and vastness that is God, and it can be overwhelming.

In our immaturity and lack of self-awareness of what is going on with our hearts, we can get very lost in chasing something we already have. There is a tension between the present and the future that must be embraced to live out the miracle that is your life. We must learn to not be so fearful of disappointment, loss, and lack and realize those things are simply reminders of what you're longing for in the first place. I don't become disappointed about things unfulfilled in my life unless I've desired them first. This means when I become self-aware that I'm focused on lack, afraid to be disappointed, or living in my loss, then all I need to do is recognize what it's pointing to! I go back to my origin and remember my promises and say to the loss, "You may be my present, but you are not my future." I laugh at the disappointment and I say, "Oh, thank you for reminding me what it is I'm passionate about and longing for." I look at my lack and I say aloud, "You've never been nor ever will be my portion!" This isn't good-vibing yourself into joy; it's acknowledging what is going on in your heart and not hiding from it but reminding yourself that though fear, disappointment, lack, and loss may be present, they aren't your future because you are an overcomer with the mind to do something about it. You've been anointed to overcome!

After that day when I was reminded about my origin with God, anytime I sat at my computer to begin writing—in full agreement with God that authoring and coaching/pastoring was what I would be about—anxiety would promptly show up asking me who I thought I was, pretending I was a writer who had something to say. But then I'd remember my origin story. I would remember that Jesus' yoke is easy and His burden is light. My work wasn't about accomplishing something, so I would never feel lack; it was about achieving because He has achieved and I'm seated in heavenly places with Him! So, I'd say to the anxiety, out loud (proclamation is your victory song), "I am a writer! I believe, so I shall speak!" And the more I did that the less I became afraid of losing something that I could never lose—my voice. I no longer feared being silenced. This is a practice I do in every life area.

God's favor is the light in which you should see yourself. You're revealed in this light so that you can see exactly who it is you are becoming. Receiving this act of kindness requires faith, because when He reveals who you are in that glorious light, you'll be doing things that are beyond your understanding. No question— it's beyond your understanding because it's His mind that you're sharing in. But always remember it's because you are loved, not so you can be loved, that He shares with you His glory.

It's very important that you embrace your humanness—the very thing that God calls good and loves—and live from that place. Avoid compartmentalizing and segregating yourself, thinking He only sees one piece of you and loves only that piece. God is reconciling you wholly back to Him. He wants every piece of you and loves all of your pieces. He's not worried about your brokenness; in fact, it's why He loves you and shares His righteousness with you. It's when you become okay with who you are presently and believe in faith that He's truly the author and perfecter of your faith that you begin to rest and discover yourself alongside Him. Your life becomes a joy and you become a joy to those around you.

This is why your testimony is not simply about where you've been; it's also very much about where you are going! God is making crooked paths straight all right, but are you noticing where it's leading you? Have you caught glimpses of your future and possessed the wisdom to align your present to get there? It's hard for us to do that when we don't know ourselves the way God knows us. And if you're like me, once I began seeing the potential of who I could become through God's eyes, I was ready to run full steam ahead, not realizing His purpose wasn't about a grand destination; rather, it was about our relationship growing and developing into its full potential.

6

GOD CAN EVEN USE A REDHEAD

I don't believe I would have had the confidence to believe I could partner with Holy Spirit in reconciling men back to God through hearing His voice if it hadn't been for my husband but also one other special person.

"Can I sit here?" I looked up to see a blue-eyed redhead staring back at me. I could tell immediately she wasn't going to take no for an answer. We ate lunch together that day and we have rarely been apart since—that is, until I moved away. And even though I've moved away, we make sure to stay in daily conversation with one another. We are way too invested in one another to simply reduce that friendship into something merely seasonal.

We always joked that our devotion to one another was like that of Ruth and Naomi's from the Bible. I, of course, was the elder of the two, not because I was wise but because I was old. That blue-eyed ginger is named Stefanie, and it has been through my relationship with her that I've experienced why embracing the prophetic nature we all have is so vital to not only myself but to the world around me. Seeing myself the way God sees me and agreeing with Heaven is certainly the vital first step in awakening your prophetic voice, but it's also very much about learning how to champion others in ways that we simply couldn't without the beautiful gift of prophecy. Together, she and I have held each other accountable to recalling who God is and what He is saying about us and our destiny. I believe that you can't truly love someone else well until you learn to love yourself well first, and I don't believe you'll ever be able to love yourself well until you receive the love that God has for you as you experience being known by God. My relationship with Stefanie is evidence that God is not only passionate about His children but even more passionate about us prophetically seeing His children through His eyes.

It was three years into my friendship with Stefanie before she told me she sang. I was shocked. This was the first I had heard of it. I had never heard her sing. I challenged her to sing for me and she pulled me into a back room and sang for me. Her voice, her courage to be known in a new way, her gift, hit my heart so hard that I began to cry as she sang. She was not just someone who could sing; she was a singer. There's a difference. It was built into the fabric of her being, and she was allowing me to hear her blatantly anointed voice. Yet, she was pulling me into a back room, almost in secret before she would sing. Naturally, I gushed about her voice in the most sincere ways. I encouraged her to not hide her voice, not that I knew if she was, but I assumed so because she only sang in front of me in private after three years of knowing her. She's not one for much attention, though, I'll give her that, but still I knew the world was waiting to hear her voice—she just had not recognized it on that level yet.

I never play the game of convincing. I am not patient enough for it, but I will believe in you until you are able to hold on to a vision for yourself. While I love to prophesy what God is saying over people, I find people really begin to possess the word being spoken over their life if they hear it and see if it for themselves. If I'm prophetically speaking into someone's life, it should be confirmation of what is already going on in their heart, though they maybe don't have the courage to believe in it. It was through Stefanie that God taught me this. He taught me that unless people can possess His words, they will never know Him or experience being known. I found leading people into hearing God for themselves was vital to help people move the mountain between what they could see and what they believed.

Right when Stefanie began to sing, I knew it would be my job to make sure she had every available opportunity to use her voice, because her voice was a gift that needed to be developed and shared. How was I going to do this? Prayer. A lot of agreeing, releasing, and praying from a place of "It will be so, God, because You've anointed it to be so!" Even though she had no idea I was interceding and prophetically declaring hope to rise up over her life, I knew this would be a great start to being a good friend for her. Not everyone will always know the depths of your love for them, but God knows!

You see, Stefanie had a very similar upbringing to mine. We weren't raised believing that God was audibly speaking or giving us insight through visions and dreams, and I was terrified to let her know that I was encountering God, seeing angels, and prophesying. In some ways, my tears as she sang to me in that little back room were in part because she exposed the worshiper within her—a worshiper I could see she was secretly nurturing and held sacred, yet I didn't have the courage at that time to reciprocate. I was unable to let her know that I had a voice that was awakening too. I was afraid to be seen as supernaturally alive and scared to be seen in this new way that God was awakening within me out of fear of being misunderstood or being rejected by one of the most important people to me. The only cure for fear of man is to love them the way God does. If perfect love is casting out fear, seeing others the way God does will cast out your fear of what they may think or believe about you. Even though they may never agree or see what you see, unity can happen between people if love, not agreement, is the common bond shared.

It wasn't long before Stefanie was invited to sing a solo in a city-wide Christmas cantata. My husband and I made it out to see her, and that was when my husband saw what I had been raving about. I remember him telling her after the performance just how incredible she was. She, of course, was polite and thankful but I think a little embarrassed. It's a little terrifying when people begin to see exactly who you are and they start believing in the potential you carry. Why? Because when people begin to believe in you, you either take responsibility for that potential or you reject it and begin to wither away in mediocrity. Either way you choose, those who believe in you are watching.

Stefanie was destined for more than just Christmas cantatas and the occasional Sunday morning worship special. The anointing on her life was visible and required development. I wasn't sure what she was specifically going to need, but I continued to pray and secretly prophesy out loud who she was and call forth everything that God had available for her. Our friendship continued to flourish.

Over the years, we shared coffee, good food, and lots of laughs. I think laughter is a cornerstone of our friendship. One of these "homemade cinnamon roll and hot coffee fueled" mornings,

Stefanie, the pillar of strength that she always is, seemed to be in need of support. I had known that she was going through personal things within her family, but circumstances had developed since I had seen her last, and if she ever needed a friend, this day was that day. She looked up at me and said, "It's days like this that you wish God was still speaking today."

I felt every muscle in my body tense. This was my moment to speak up so she could experience God's love. I felt my throat tighten, but my passion and belief in people hearing God's voice was stronger than my fear, so without overthinking it I responded with, "I believe He is speaking today. Would you like to hear what He has to say?" She studied the sincerity in my eyes for only a moment and then said yes. Then, like everyone who is passionate about the gift of prophecy, I told her I'd come back the next day and share with her what God was saying. I ran to my car with my tail between my legs. I literally told her God could speak and then left her in her pain.

The next day I went to her house as promised. Nervous, probably not unlike how she felt when she sang in front of me, I started off simply praying for her, and then I began to prophesy. I won't share all that, but I will say that it's a word she and I recall often as a remembrance of not only who God is for her but His promises about where she is going outside of the circumstantial evidence. After that intimate moment with my best friend, I went on to tell her of the countless prophetic testimonies that I had been experiencing that had led me to know God is not only good but He is speaking loud and clear today. I told her about my class that Pastor Jay had given me so that I could lead people into hearing God for themselves, and she asked to sign up even though she didn't attend my church.

This was the moment when I stopped being so afraid of using my voice prophetically. I risked being misunderstood and didn't entertain fear of man, so I spoke. And I have to say, it's when everything began to change for me. But I want you to notice that I didn't speak up because I was proving to Stefanie that God still spoke today. I was motivated by love and compassion. My friend was hurting; she needed to know where God was, and I was compelled to get past my fears and lead her to the One who could really help her in ways that I just wouldn't know how otherwise. The Holy Spirit is the great unifier. You don't have to experience someone else's pain to have an impact in someone's life; all you need is compassion and a knowing that God is really, really good, and Holy Spirit does the rest.

Never lead with your gifts; rather, lead with gratitude for the person you're serving. You'll learn that the ability to grow in relationship with people is the most impressive gift God ever gave you. Your gifts are only tools to help you love others in impressive ways.

If you could have a star student in a church class, it would be Stefanie. It had nothing to do with being extra gifted; it only had to do with hunger! She was hungry to intimately know God. She was beginning to experience her holy union with God through Holy Spirit and was starting to see, hear, and know not only the plans He had for her but know God was good and that she could take big risks with her life because He was with her! Others in the class were having incredible breakthrough as well, but Stefanie was taking God at His word, and she was soaring. With prophetic images God had given her of equipping others through worship, she auditioned for and made the worship team at my church. In no time, she began to lead a team of her own where she learned the ins and outs of leading others who felt called to worship. Her voice was awakened, but still she was barely scratching the surface.

After several years of leading locally, still leaning on the promises and declarations that God had spoken over her, she auditioned to become a worship team member of a church plant that was branching from one of the most influential, internationally known worship teams. This worship team would be directly influenced and mentored by some of the most talented global musicians; it was an opportunity for Stefanie to learn from the best. Audition submissions flooded in, including one with Stefanie's name on it. She got a callback for a live audition. At the audition, they called her name to be the first to sing. She was nervous; she even says that she started off pretty rough, but soon she found her voice amongst the nerves and simply released it!

Sitting in the audience were the audition candidates, the worship pastor, and the pastors of the church plant with their baby. After she sang, the worship pastor asked everyone to come and look at the baby. A large, half-dollar sized drop of oil had manifested on the baby's head. Stefanie, remember, was raised in a church community where that was unseen and not believed in. She walked over to the baby and said the fragrance from the oil was so strong, that she had never smelled anything like it before. It wasn't only picked up by smell, but the fragrance itself was experienced. She said it was as if you could smell it, taste it, hear it as if the oil were alive. She was stunned. She assumed it had been the hour-long pre-worship they had before auditions began that set the atmosphere for miracles and wonders; she never expected that it had anything to do with her.

Four hours later the auditions wrapped. The worship pastor pulled Stefanie off to the side and told her that her audition tape was not good. It was so not good that he only watched three minutes out of four total videos that had been submitted, but before finishing his list of callbacks he prayed and asked Holy Spirit to highlight anyone he may have missed. Stefanie's rejected audition video was highlighted. He went back to listen to her submission, and sure enough it wasn't her that was the issue, it was the guitarist who he said wasn't technically at her level yet. He told her that he knew he needed to start auditions off with her because she was anointed to set the tone for the auditions that were to follow, and that oil from Heaven on the baby's head was the manifestation of the anointing that God had placed uniquely on her voice. He went on to tell her that whether it was on their team or somewhere else, she needed to be saying yes to her voice and using it.

Talk about affirmation! Stefanie had to travel out of state to do the live audition and was staying at our house, so it was a special moment getting to watch her walk out of her audition so monumentally impacted by what God did to affirm what she carried. You can imagine she was overwhelmed by God. After getting into the car she struggled to even speak, and of course as she shared what had happened during the audition I became a blubbering mess. My husband met our emotion with the remark, "Well, if God can use the voice of an ass to get man's attention, as the classic Bible story goes, it's no surprise God can even use a redhead!" We all burst out laughing!

There are seasons when you will have no one believing in you; you may even have people mocking you. But those are the tests required so your feet can stand firm in who God is saying you are. I believe Stefanie always had visions of her singing, likely from the time she was small. I believe she always knew deep down that it wasn't just that she could sing but that her voice was equipped uniquely to bridge people into the presence of God; maybe she just didn't know how to translate those giant imaginings into practically walking it out. It doesn't matter. Eventually, God will send someone along who will see what God has placed on your life. If you'll be open-hearted and brave and not shrink back, someone will rise up and agree with God's belief in you. Even if it means pulling one person into a back room so you can sing for them; or even if it means declaring what you believe, high-tailing it out of there, and then returning the next day to honor your belief in the desires God has placed in your heart. They will remind you of who you are when you're in doubt. They'll recall the promises that God has spoken over you! And most importantly, they will pray. They will pray when that's all there to do. But we don't wait for these people to come along before we use our voice!

Stefanie and I have been in a friendship for over ten years. About seven of those years we have been actively cultivating a prophetic friendship—meaning we remind one another of who God says we are; we prophesy over one another; we walk hand in hand together through the hard stuff, not just the fun stuff; and we carry hope for one another when our hope is fading. God will send someone, but will you risk being seen and known so that they can partner with Heaven to champion you into your destiny? Will you be bold and speak out what Heaven is saying about someone who needs to hear God? Gifts are most profound when they are wrapped up in loving long-term relationships, not just the "wham, bam, hope that helps and see ya later ma'am" kind of love.

All of us have a voice that needs to be awakened. God has placed His vision for our lives uniquely inside your voice so that, like Him, we will powerfully look to the void and speak out the imaginings of God's heart! With a "let it be so" attitude, we create beautiful things out of nothing. It starts with an awakened voice that is declaring the heart of Heaven into the earth. It's the new sound coming from you that the earth has been groaning for.

7

INVITING JESUS TO THE PARTY

I learned very quickly what it looks like when people begin to operate freely in the gifts without truly knowing God as their Father. I learned quickly what it looks like when an orphaned people filter real encounters with God through their woundedness and fears and then begin to project that onto everyone around them. When people operate in the gifts without remembering who God is and they don't know God's heart, they begin to filter their encounters through their wounds and judgements or their religious traditions. Unfortunately, they display a picture of God that is not accurate.

This was when I understood that before I could simply teach people how to discern God's voice, I had to guide them through a biblical foundation of Jesus Christ—because He is the full picture of who God the Father truly is and who they too will reflect as a new creation. Any experience that doesn't reflect the heart of Jesus needs to be examined closer or tossed out completely. Jesus is our scale on which everything is measured.

When I began to stir people's belief that they actually do know God's voice, people began walking into breakthrough moments with Holy Spirit! There were no formulas or pre-scripted plans, no long hours of prayer or begging God to speak to us. It was simply unity among us in our belief that we are one with God and He is speaking today! I'm talking about hard cases—fragmented, broken people, even Baptists who believed they were too depraved for God to speak to them were having sincere experiences that shifted their mindsets about who God was and who they were to God! I also began to observe that if we were in a group setting, community began to form in a very powerful way. People were not only prophetically confessing what God was speaking over them, but they began to get prophetic glimpses of one another too, and they started holding each other accountable to the word of God that was being seen and spoken. Once beggars, now they were upright and praying as children who were postured securely beside their all-powerful Father!

I came to passionately believe that everyone is prophetic simply because I believe Jesus demonstrated walking out a prophetic lifestyle. I believe that every miracle moment that Jesus performed was a prophetic act testifying to who God is and who the world is to God! It's said in John 21:25 that Jesus performed so many miracles that not even all the books in the world could contain them. If all those acts are prophetic acts of God speaking of His nature, revealing His ways, then He has a lot to say! And we are included in the group Jesus described in John 14:12—believers who would do what He does and even greater things—so God is continuing to speak through us today! It appears as if God may be a jabber box, but it's with His voice that He draws us out and back into His arms, revealing to the world that He is alive!

God created us to know His voice, and it was through prophetic encounters that I was reconciled back to His amazing love. I believe all the gifts reveal the nature of God to us, but the prophetic creates a place of being known where we find wholeness and healing, we find family and community, we experience salvation only found in Jesus.

John 10:27 says that His sheep know his voice. It is through hearing His voice that I believe my children's children will inherit a legacy as a people who are known for walking with God.

My belief that all are prophetic in nature applies to children as well. My boys walk in the prophetic very naturally, and it's beautiful. Watching them is actually how I learn quite a lot about the prophetic gift. When I began growing in my understanding that God is speaking to all of us today in unique ways, I did what a lot of us who begin to embrace the prophetic do—I went out on what is called a "treasure hunt." A treasure hunt is when a group of people pray for Holy Spirit to give them specifics about a person and the details about where they are. They then write those details down on a piece of paper that they will later show the person as proof that God wants to speak to them specifically, so much so that He gave details about them prior to ever meeting them. It's essentially creating an opportunity for people to know they are known and loved by a very alive God who is speaking today. It's a fun equipping exercise.

I wanted my boys to grow in confidence that they too can hear God's voice and practice loving people in radical ways, so I took them on a treasure hunt at a local church that does it every Saturday night in Springfield, Missouri. Before hitting the streets, all the participants prayed, including my two boys who each held a pencil and their own piece of paper to scribble down the pictures or words they felt Holy Spirit was sharing with them. I looked to my right and my youngest son, who was probably five at the time, was drawing a bunch of upside-down crosses. I gasped in silence. I hoped no one was looking. Here we were sitting in a church, praying for Holy Spirit to speak to us, and my son was over here feverishly drawing upside-down crosses all over his page as if he was possessed by some other spirit that was not holy. I looked to my left and my oldest son was drawing skulls and crossbones.

I tried to focus—I prayed and heard a specific location where we were supposed to go and that I'd find a woman in a red sweatshirt there. Shuffling my boys' papers behind mine, I drove my boys and a friend to the location I felt we would find our "treasure." Immediately upon opening my car door, I could hear a woman screaming and crying out. I turned and there was the woman with a red sweatshirt, on her knees crying out. I remember being so nervous. This woman was in real emotional pain, and I had no way of knowing how she'd respond to a group of us approaching her.

As a side note, I have never been afraid to let my boys be around brokenness. Because of that, they have seen Jesus countless times free the captives, heal the sick, and deliver the oppressed. They not only know Jesus loves them, they've seen Him love others in action, which only builds their trust. In their time of need, and they will have times of need, they know the name to call out to!

I approached and showed her my list that met all of her descriptions. I told her I was just at a church praying and God told me about her specifically and where to find her and that's why I showed up. She sat there stunned, wiping away tears. I asked her what was going on, and she began to describe in detail the brokenness in her life when a man walked up, an apparent friend of hers, and stood beside her as she shared her story.

After a few minutes, before we began to pray for her, my little boy tugged on my shirt and pointed discreetly at the man standing behind her. The black t-shirt that he was wearing was covered in upside-down crosses, skulls, and crossbones. I smiled and was reminded that I can certainly trust that my kids know God's voice.

As our friend who was with us began to powerfully pray over the woman we were ministering to, I asked Jake and Jackson, my boys, if they'd like to lead the prayer over the guy standing with her. They agreed. My boys went through the whole thing. They showed him their papers, how God knew he was going to show up tonight and God had something to say to him, and then the boys laid hands on this man and prayed with power. When they finished praying we hugged them. As we walked away we could hear the man shouting in the streets that God had sent people to pray for him. Throughout the streets you could hear the man shouting that God was with him. It was a very powerful moment for the people we ministered to, but it was also a learning moment for me that my children hear God's voice and I need to trust that God is not offended by the things we often are. My children today have ministered to hundreds of people prophetically, and God often gives them vivid dreams and incredible visions for our family's future. We have a family journal that we place these words and promises in to so that we can steward them well.

Holy Spirit is in the business of revealing God the Father to us, not through sheer logic or persuasion by charismatic speakers but by revealing Himself to us in an infinite number of supernatural ways, which we often generally categorize as hearing God's voice. God is speaking to us today in incredible ways, each way as unique as fingerprints.

If anyone reading this book believes they've never had a "prophetic encounter," then they don't understand the prophetic moment that led them to salvation. The moment when you "felt," "heard," "believed"—however you describe the moment you knew you needed Christ as your Savior—was a prophetic moment when you experienced God's voice that led you to repentance! Hearing God's voice is far more than the reason of salvation—it's so we can know God intimately and taste and see the incredible life He wants us to have with and through Him.

Romans 8:19-22 says that the earth is groaning for the sons of God to be made manifest. This simply means that God gifted the earth with us for a reason! Through a relationship with God, we will see the plans He has for us. Upon being awakened and enlightened by Holy Spirit, you will do things far beyond what even Jesus did—His words, not mine! The earth is waiting for you to reveal the likeness of God in which you were designed.

I believe every human has had prophetic experiences with God, but they either don't have the wisdom or maturity to understand it and they dismiss it or they believe they've experienced something supernatural and so they worship their encounters. The prophetic gift becomes an idol that they worship like any other idol in their life, making them unbalanced and loonical (a word I created to describe the process of becoming loony). Then you have those who just want to be "normal," so they reject all of it and the people who believe in it too. What they don't understand is they are shutting down the very form of communication that God uses to mature us into His love and likeness. They may have forgotten that Jesus is our standard for what is normal, not culture or doctrines. I believe this is why Paul says of all the gifts, you should desire the prophetic (see 1 Cor. 14:1). To embrace a prophetic lifestyle is to know and be known by God!

If you think God doesn't already know that humanity is prone to manufacture hype or be a fickle flake, then you haven't read your Bible. He knows how to mature us through those things. He's been doing it since the beginning of time. And if you're offended by God's process with humanity, then you will continue to be blinded by the gigantic plank in your eye and likely never taste true wisdom that can only come from Holy Spirit. Growing with God requires trading off the old for the new, and you can't partake in that outside of humility and keeping your eyes on Jesus.

My favorite story is of a woman who was actually not in our small group but a small group member led me to her. She believed she could not hear from God because she heard multiple voices in her head already. She had been struggling with hearing voices for a long while and she was exhausted. As tears ran down her face, she asked me to help her hear from God, but insisted that she couldn't. I had no strategy or technique, but God is good and He wants to reveal Himself to us all.

When you operate in the gifts from a childlike posture, trusting in God's goodness, you need no pre-written plan or scripted prayer because it's not about you, it's about Him! When you simply abide in sonship (and daughtership) and let Holy Spirit reveal how truly loved they are, you discover the very power that raises the dead, heals the sick, and the supernatural kindness that leads men to repentance.

I sat next to the woman whom I had never met before that night and told her not to worry about all the voices; she will know Jesus when she hears Him. She insisted she wouldn't because the other voices were so loud, and my response was, "No need to silence the other voices; let's just invite Jesus to the party." I asked her to close her eyes, and all I said was, "Holy Spirit, come!" Within seconds of me asking Holy Spirit to come, her body relaxed and her countenance lightened. Tears rolled down her face, and she smiled so softly. I knew she was meeting Jesus. I asked her if she wanted to share what she was experiencing, and she began to describe a scene of when she was a small child, a memory that she had forgotten about that brought her incredible peace. I then asked her to close her eyes again because Jesus wanted to speak with her about that moment. She closed her eyes, more tears came, and she shared the most intimate, reconciling conversation Jesus was having with her.

I asked her about the other voices, and she realized that they were not there. When she recognized that Jesus had silenced the loud chatter in her head in mere seconds, you could see a supernatural rest come over her that she had not experienced in a long while. She had just encountered the Prince of Peace. She messaged me several days later, and she told me that she had not heard a single voice since that moment. She was so encouraged by that experience that she ended up buying one of my devotionals and giving it to her therapist, who then began to use it with her patients.

Personal prophetic encounters with Jesus propel breakthrough. It's the moment when you are filled with insight and strategy that ignites life-giving hope! Breakthrough is the manifestation of remembrance that you and God are one, and in that moment of surrender it doesn't matter what your circumstance is—it bows its knee to God! Holy Spirit uses these moments to create anchor points in our soul that become the very foundation that matures us into the abundant life we were destined for!

Breakthrough is not something we are necessarily waiting for because it's built into our identity. It's something we practice. It becomes a lifestyle of our faith. As an overcomer, Jesus has created us to be walking breakthroughs for everyone in our lives, including ourselves. I just so happen to do it through the prophetic gift. Sometimes I prophesy God's heart over people, but I would say 80 percent of the time the way I create breakthrough moments for people is by helping them to hear what God is saying over them for themselves. Almost every day, I get to see intimate moments between God and His people being reconciled through the prophetic gift. I thank God He chose me for the calling of inviting the life of the party, Jesus, to people so they can experience not just how good God is but also how good they are too!

POWERFUL PEOPLE ARE A PROPHETIC PEOPLE!

When Jesus came to the region of Caesarea Philippi, he asked his disciples, "Who do people say the Son of Man is?" They replied, "Some say John the Baptist; others say Elijah; and still others, Jeremiah or one of the prophets." "But what about you?" he asked. "Who do you say I am?" Simon Peter answered, "You are the Messiah, the Son of the living God." Jesus replied, "Blessed are you, Simon son of Jonah, for this was not revealed to you by flesh and blood, but by my Father in heaven. And I tell you that you are Peter, and on this rock I will build my church, and the gates of Hades will not overcome it. I will give you the keys of the kingdom of heaven; whatever you bind on earth will be bound in heaven, and whatever you loose on earth will be loosed in heaven" (Matthew 16:13-19).

During a discussion with His disciples, Jesus asked *"Who do you say I am?"* Peter answered *"You are the Messiah, the Son of the living God."* There was a lot of speculation about who Jesus was.

By simply observing Him, people assumed a lot of things, but Peter wasn't simply going off of what he observed; he was enlightened by Holy Spirit. Jesus said, *"Blessed are you, Simon son of Jonah, for this was not revealed to you by flesh and blood, but by my Father in heaven."* Jesus then went on to prophesy over Peter. He described how Peter was known in Heaven and would be known on earth—faithful and powerful.

Peter's faith in Jesus was built upon revelation given to him from God. I believe this is a perfect example of what exactly God wants us to discern, enlightened by Holy Spirit—the revelation of how we are known by God.

God's family is a people of sight, of vision. They are able to not only look into the mirror and see what God sees, but it's okay that they see their limitations also and embrace them. They know Holy Spirit is who empowers them. How do you think Jesus hung around those twelve all the time? Do you think it was because He knew their Myers-Briggs personality assessment and related accordingly? Or was it because they were all theologically sound and really intelligent? That's hilarious.

Jesus saw all their faults and their flaws, all their misinterpretations and shallow understanding, yet He embraced them. He didn't keep them at arm's length because they weren't "safe" people. He rebuked them when they spoke out of fear and ignorance, but He wasn't so concerned with them saying the right things all the time and sounding correct. Shoot, they were sleeping on the job, competing with one another, and concerned with their reputations. They were just like us. Jesus was able to push past the immature, the religious rhetoric, and find purity. Discerning the spirit, Jesus knew people the way they were known in Heaven and could easily see any spirit that was coming against their own knowledge of that truth.

Holy Spirit has enabled you to see. Practice seeing people how God sees them. Grow in your love for people so that you love even strangers the same way you love those closest to you. Discern the spirits that are coming against their knowledge of who they are in Christ. Otherwise, you will be constantly offended by everyone's lack and limits, and you will grow powerless, choosing disconnection over connection.

Did you know that Jesus has set you free from what you don't know? The prophetic gift is not so you can always have the answers. He set you free from trying to be right or trying to "get right." It's His righteousness that you've taken on. It's His mind that you share in. The pressure has never been on you; that would be self-righteousness. Your job is to stop trying to look right and simply abide in His righteousness. It's from this place you begin to look past other people's lack and limits and Holy Spirit begins to show you what's true! You then become the only *yes* in a room full of *no*. You begin to push past the blazing accusations that have been formed against every single human, and you become the one who stops and takes notice.

When everyone else is saying *no* and putting up boundaries and keeping one another at arm's length, you become the one who says with their actions that they deserve to be known, regardless of their personality assessments, their tattoos, their sexual preference, their faith, gender, or skin color. Don't you see? This is the power that God gave you—to see the world and love the world the way He does. It has nothing to do with agreement with their thoughts and their ways but everything to do with agreement with God's thoughts. Holy Spirit enables us to walk like Jesus did, revealing that they are loved and known by the living God and can be empowered by Holy Spirit to walk in something new!

8

LEARNING TO DISCERN

As I mentioned, when I began walking out a prophetic lifestyle, I didn't even know what the word *prophetic* meant. I remember being invited to a Sunday morning church service by a teenager my husband and I had previously youth pastored, and we agreed to go. The pastor said that his message was going to be on prophecy and discerning the voice of God. What felt like electricity ran across my body. I was all ears. As he began defining things I had never heard of, like words of wisdom and words of knowledge, tears filled my eyes. I knew Holy Spirit was guiding me and leading me to the community I needed to get me where I needed to go. It would be that very pastor and that very community that launched me into my calling.

Regardless of whether you feel you discern God's voice easily or you feel you've never experienced it, you will not delay God's plans for your life. Hebrews 12:2 says that Jesus is the author and perfecter of our faith! That says to me that those who call upon the name of the Lord, who seek to know God, will not only find God but will see and know that He has His hand in yours and is leading you to everything you need so you can succeed. In Christ, our only outcome is victory! Right in this moment, God knows the communities you need so you can flourish. God knows the resources you need to pull you into great things with Him. Holy Spirit will stop at nothing short of you seeing the victory that was and is and is to come!

One of the biggest things I run into when equipping people in the prophetic and discerning Holy Spirit is the question, "How do I know if it's God I'm discerning?" Unfortunately, because of bad theology and bad identity, this question comes up all the time. People have been taught that they are no good and they can't trust in a union with God let alone believe that God trusts in them. I mean, we compromise our own internal integrity so often—meaning we make promises to ourselves and then break them, repeatedly letting our own hearts down—so how can we even begin to trust in the discernment that God has built into our beings? True discernment begins with believing that God trusts us enough that He shares not only secrets with us—He shares His confidence, so that we may discern ways His perfect love can operate in our lives or the lives of others. It's hard for us to reconcile that God speaks to sinners! But He does, He is, and it's how He is maturing us into functioning in His likeness. As a general rule of thumb, it's easier when we simply keep our eyes on the hope of glory—Christ, who is in us! (See Colossians 1:27.)

You'll know if it's Holy Spirit giving you prophetic insight or wisdom because Holy Spirit convicts you of sin and righteousness (see John 16:8). Remember, sin is not the behavior; behavior is the symptom of a lie that is believed. Sin is your belief when you've forgotten who God is for you in that moment and who you are to God in that moment. What you believe will always empower something. Belief will either empower the remembrance of who God is and what He has said to you regardless of circumstance, or it will empower a lie. Any life area where you are empowering lies with your belief is sin. Discernment from Holy Spirit will be picking up on the lies that are coming against the knowledge of God, and you'll be discerning what's actually true (righteousness) too. It's not one or the other; it's both!

I hear a lot of people say they have the gift of discernment, but when I hear what they are discerning I quickly know if it's God they are hearing, accusations they are agreeing with, or if it's simply reading people. Discernment given by Holy Spirit will always have sound understanding attached to solutions. Why? Because the spirit of prophecy is Jesus Christ and Christ is a victor.

I cringe when I hear someone say they are gifted with godly discernment and then they begin to tell me all the dirty secrets and all the warnings they are receiving about someone. I can tell by their fruit what spirit they are hearing. If it's God, it'll look a whole lot like power and love and less like division and gossip. I'm not saying God doesn't warn us so that we can approach circumstances with wisdom in dealing with other people. But while you may not be led to approach every single person, if God gives you insight, He will give you promises and prophetic strategies to declare over them, even if it's from afar. If you've stewarded discernment correctly, you won't be left feeling anything but hope for that individual and their circumstance, and nothing less should be coming from your mouth. How could it be anything different when it's Jesus who is the source of your information?

One time I was sitting at a favorite restaurant, and while waiting for the food to arrive I looked up and saw the girl who was working behind the cash register. Without any asking, Holy Spirit gave me complete insight about what was going on in her current life. I saw that her father was very sick and in a hospital bed. On top of worrying about her father's fading health, she was financially carrying the burden in her family, and she was concerned about paying her bills. I actually saw that she had a low amount of money in the bank, and she was hoping she would be able to cover her bills. By outward appearances, she didn't look like someone who was worrying. Simple observation told me that she did her job above and beyond and was excellent at customer service, but Holy Spirit was giving me insight into her internal world—she was stressed and barely holding it together emotionally.

As I received all this information in the form of what I call a knowing experience (no visions, just a knowing of information that comes), I sat there watching her, empathizing. I was experiencing her fear. I just continued to sit and stare. Holy Spirit nudged and asked me to go pray with her. I said no. That's when a familiar holy correction hit my heart. I heard Holy Spirit say, "I don't share the secrets of My children's hearts for your entertainment." I mean, God's not spilling the tea about someone's life just so I can sit and gawk into their life. Holy Spirit empowers us to love really, really well, way beyond anything we could ever do—hence the prophetic insight. The gifts are meant to be given away and to demonstrate God's incredible power and love, and it's never any more complicated than that. I wish I could say that I got up and went and prayed for her. I walked out of that restaurant without ever going to her, and I missed an opportunity that God had empowered me to take.

Lesson learned: Discernment is about being empowered, not being entitled. You are not entitled to information about anyone's life. God graces us with wisdom and insight so we are empowered to shift external and internal atmospheres. It's what Jesus called advancing the Kingdom of God—bringing Heaven to earth. Discernment has power and frees people from the fear and bondage that they are repeating and reliving every single day! I love what Shawn Bolz says: "True love can see people as though they were never separated from God, and then true lovers of God treat them that way." If perfect love truly casts out all fear, then discernment and prophetic insight is love's tactical operation that results in fear being cast out. I tell you, after that moment I got over myself real quick and realized God didn't awaken my prophetic voice so that I could sit and observe from the sidelines; He did it so that I could jump in the race and not only win but push people ahead of me so they could experience winning too!

God is maturing His people from being selective hearers to excellent listeners. Holy Spirit is maturing us into people who are present and fully engaged in life! It's like a spouse who has been accused of "selective hearing"—only hearing when it's convenient— choosing to stay present and fully engaged within the relationship, exchanging dialogue, dreams, and desires.

As a coach, I often ask people what they believe people see when looking at them. What do people walk away knowing about them? Essentially, what they are experiencing is what they will begin to be known for. What they should be experiencing is someone who is present, is walking out truth (not perfection), and is engaged with every life area. It doesn't have to look orderly, but it should look like living.

In each life area, we all have spheres of influence. As a mom, I have authority and influence in the relationships with my children. As a wife, I champion my man. I remind him of his potential and recall where he's come from and what God's promised to him! My husband uses his authority to push me out further than I could go on my own and influences me by reminding me who I am. I am a life coach with a global clientele, and I have a committed responsibility to walk through life with them, sometimes as a pastor and sometimes as a coach. As a woman, I have an influence with women. You get the picture. We all inherited responsibilities that need to be accepted. That's a problem for most of us because we don't want to take on responsibilities. Some want responsibilities, but they are waiting for permission. I see a lot of women struggle with that one. But it's important to understand that we've been empowered by Holy Spirit to be experts in every life area that we are immediately called to. We're not born experts, but we are transforming into learned experts, and it's never outside of relationships with others. We must choose to face life and live it from a place of power and love, leading from a sound mind. What does this look like?

As humans, we are to submit ourselves to one another, grow in community with one another, and learn to equip and encourage people into being powerful through meaningful relationships. But it requires that we begin to view people in the right light.

Second Corinthians 5:16-21 lays it out perfectly:

> *So from now on we regard no one from a worldly point of view. Though we once regarded Christ in this way, we do so no longer. Therefore, if anyone is in Christ, the new creation has come: The old has gone, the new is here! All this is from God, who reconciled us to himself through Christ and gave us the ministry of reconciliation: that God was reconciling the world to himself in Christ, not counting people's sins against them. And he has committed to us the message of reconciliation. We are therefore*

Christ's ambassadors, as though God were making his appeal through us. We implore you on Christ's behalf: Be reconciled to God. God made him who had no sin to be sin for us, so that in him we might become the righteousness of God.

I tell my boys all the time, when you grow older you will meet some beautiful young women who don't know that they don't have to wear short shorts to get your attention. They won't know they don't have to give you permission with their body in order to gain affection from you. You will need to exercise self-control and honor them even when they don't know how to honor themselves. You will need to see them beyond what they are presenting, far beyond, and honor them for who you know they are truly—a woman created in the image of God who deserves to be treated equally and deserves to be known. True power is exercising self-control and seeing people the way God sees them. True power and freedom isn't being able to do whatever you want, whenever you want. True power comes from choosing self-control when you don't have to. Freedom will always honor someone or something. Powerful people see people in a different light than what is presented, resulting in honoring people even when they don't know how to value and honor themselves.

It doesn't take a spiritual gift to point out the negative in a person. It doesn't take someone wise beyond their years to point out people's flaws. It's the wise who see past behavior and see potential. It's the spiritually gifted, rooted in God's heart, who are able to call out what isn't yet, as if it already is. God has been doing that with mankind since the very beginning. He's been calling us a holy priesthood, His own children before any of us ever knew Him!

God is all powerful because He could destroy us, but He chose to love and reconcile us back to Him. Think about it. God's grace would have no value if it wasn't for the fact that He didn't have to extend it to us. God is above us and beyond us, yet He gives us access to Him in every way. Through His choice to offer us reconciliation by way of viewing us and calling us by His name even before we truly knew Him, we can say that God is all powerful! And by observing Jesus, who came to reveal the Father, we can say that He is the epitome of love.

God's people are not only powerful because they say yes to who they are in God, which requires self-control to say yes to that vision, reality, and truth a million times per day. They are also in the process of prophetically seeing others the way God sees them. They are not just going around, willy-nilly prophesying over people. As they engage in meaningful relationships within their sphere of influence (family, neighbors, friends, community), they are essentially saying yes a million times to who God says others are, too. God's people remind others, they pray for them, they write it down and make it plain. This is the way God has designed us to change the world—through relationships that are built around the way He sees His creation, His children!

I want to add this: No one is more of an expert on your life than you are. Be awakened to your true relationship with God and live from that union. You are not God's project; you are His child. This is not about behavior; it's about love. He's invested all of Heaven into you and through Holy Spirit has given you access to see and hear and know that you are good and can do impossible things if you simply believe in the Word of God that He is speaking over your life.

It's time that you begin to shape the gift of life that God gave you by seeing what He sees, by speaking out what He is speaking, and by practicing being the minister of reconciliation you are—not only with others but with yourself as well! Be reconciled! Be whole! Be free! By the power and by the Spirit that has been vested in me, I pronounce that you, the Bride, have the ability to see, hear, and know God in ways that you've never known before! I declare that you and your children will be known as a people who walked with the living God. May your life be a living testimony that God is good and that you are known by God!

Next is a devotional including built-in prophetic hearing moments so that you can begin to prophetically declare who God is revealing you to be! I encourage you to work your way through, share your visions and insights with one another, and start taking back the responsibilities that have been placed in your life that you've been avoiding for too long! Today is the day that the Lord has made; let's rejoice and be glad, because He's empowered you with Holy Spirit to do something new with this day! Let's start shaping our day by awakening our prophetic voice and declaring that today will be a good day!

AWAKENING
YOUR
PROPHETIC
VOICE

Devotional and Activations

I believe we were created from good soil. In fact, when God declared man was good, He did so with the breath of life. Matthew 13:23 says, *"But the seed falling on good soil refers to someone who hears the word and understands it. This is the one who produces a crop, yielding a hundred, sixty or thirty times what was sown."*

You were created from good soil, and you were designed to know your Creator. You are good soil. Your heart is a fertile place in which God can plant seeds of faith that will grow into fully mature spiritual fruit (see Gal. 5:22). Your life was designed to yield abundance because God placed His Word, Jesus Christ, in you. God's plan was always to give man divine family roots, a plan conceived before creation ever took its first breath. The birth of humanity testifies to the wisdom of God's creation plan.

> *But the seed falling on good soil refers to someone who hears the word and understands it. This is the one who produces a crop, yielding a hundred, sixty or thirty times what was sown* (Matthew 13:23).

In this workbook, we are going to open the eyes of our hearts and engage with God so we can grow in His truth. We will imagine, dream, listen, and see. When Holy Spirit speaks to us, teaches us, guides us, and shows us incredible things, our lives yield Heaven's abundance on earth. We will reveal the living God and His great love for the world.

In the following study, you will complete "Digging Deeper" lessons designed to help you dig in the Bible to nourish your soul and remind you of who God is and who you are to God. At the end of each lesson, you will have a Hearing Moment—an opportunity to pray, engage Holy Spirit, and experience hearing and seeing how God truly sees you. In John 10:27, Jesus says, *"My sheep listen to my voice; I know them, and they follow me."* During the Hearing Moment, you will learn to listen to God's voice and receive strength from His words.

When you allow Holy Spirit to illuminate your heart with God's voice and paint your mind with images of a destiny that God has planned for you, unbelief, doubt, and worry will lose their influence over your heart and mind. Holy Spirit will stir up your faith and you will be known as someone who walks with God. The faith He will sow into your heart and mind throughout this study will sprout dreams in some of you, and others will receive divine innovations or creative solutions to problems so that you can receive freedom, just as Paul shared in Second Corinthians 3:17.

I pray the seeds, the words I have cast upon these pages, are sown deep within your heart. And for the seeds that Holy Spirit has already sown within you, I ask for these words to fall like rain so the life that has been planted within you will awaken in the glory of the Son, Jesus Christ.

All of creation is groaning for you to realize who you are! Are you ready to grow and produce?

LESSON 1

IN THE BEGINNING

Digging Deeper

There is a big difference between *knowing about* someone and *knowing* someone. I remember one of the first few times I began to see Ben, my husband of now 13 years, around campus and other various places. He walked into freshman orientation class wearing a Hawaiian mesh shirt, khaki shorts, and sandals that he wore with socks—though he denies he ever wore socks and sandals together. He did! I was so drawn to the way he entered into the classroom with confidence and self-assuredness. After seeing him in class, I soon began asking around about him. After hearing so many stories about him, I was enticed to know him myself. Five months later, he was down on one knee asking me to marry him.

The stories I had heard about Ben couldn't compare to my firsthand experience of Ben. I fell in love with one of the most adoring and intentional people I have ever met. With each passing day, there are depths to Ben that are still unfolding to me. He absolutely fascinates me. As we grow together in this marriage, we are being fused together into a oneness that can only come from being rooted in a firsthand experience and knowledge of one another that includes trust, forgiveness, and first and foremost love. Marriage is much like our relationship with God!

What do you know about the nature of God? What is He really like?

Circle the attributes that you have been taught about God.

Thoughtful   Logical   Fatherly

Powerful   Responsible   Pleasant

Patient   Jealous   Distant

Emotional   Leader   Loyal

Devoted   Imaginative   Rigid

Rebellious   Listener   Enthusiastic

Competitive   Impatient   Intolerant

Wise   Happy   Optimistic

Funny   Angry

(add any that aren't listed)

List the attributes of God that you have experienced:

_____

_____

_____

_____

_____

_____

_____

_____

_____

_____

_____

In Hosea 4:6, we see that God cried out because He declared that His very own people don't know Him. In this particular verse, "to know" is from the Hebrew word *yada*, and it means to know by firsthand experience (Strong's #H3045). Not only were the people turning away from God because they did not believe, but the priests were also falling into idol worship. If you continue reading the passage, it goes on to say that their lack of firsthand knowledge of God would affect their future generations.

> "My people are being destroyed because they don't know me."
> —Hosea 4:6, NLT

Our intimate knowledge of God will impact our future generations, too! There is no way around it. Let's grow from assuming we know God's character to a true knowledge gained through experiencing a relationship with our heavenly Father! You were created to do so!

Read these verses:

> *Nothing in all creation is hidden from God's sight. Everything is uncovered and laid bare before the eyes of him to whom we must give account* (Hebrews 4:13).

> *Then the man and his wife heard the sound of the Lord God as he was walking in the garden in the cool of the day, and they hid from the Lord God among the trees of the garden. But the Lord God called to the man, "Where are you?" He answered, "I heard you in the garden, and I was afraid because I was naked; so I hid." And he said, "Who told you that you were naked? Have you eaten from the tree that I commanded you not to eat from?"* (Genesis 3:8-11)

1 From what we know, had Adam ever experienced the judgment of God before hiding from Him in Genesis 3:8?

○ Yes or ○ No

2 Why was Adam's first reaction to hide?

3 How much of what you know about God is based on personal experience (firsthand knowledge) or on knowing about Him (secondhand knowledge)? Does what you know about God cause you to hide from Him? Explain.

How could Adam, who knew God, or the Israelites, who experienced God's tangible devotion over and over again, turn away from Him? Simply, when our aim isn't rooted and grounded in the great I AM, satan the accuser will shake and divide our hearts and minds. Our identities must be established in His identity. Jesus enabled us to enter into an incredible union with God so that our *identity was changed* and we were given a new name. Unless our origin begins in Christ, our identity statement, our I AM, will be rooted outside of truth and we will live in a reality that God never created nor intended for us! Our Father is calling His children home. He's pursuing us and giving us more than we deserve or could ever imagine. Aren't you ready to hear and see and live out that reality to the fullest?

Think for a moment about the power of your very own testimony. Revelation 12:11 says that we overcome the accuser through the blood of the Lamb (Jesus Christ) and the word of our testimony. Our testimony is a declaration of a first-hand knowledge of the living God in our lives. Our testimony ignites faith when God's relationship with humanity is revealed through our individual stories. The praise and proclamation of our very own relationship with our Savior is so powerful. He has interwoven Himself into us and given us the authority to overcome everything the accuser can throw at us!

Over the next eight lessons, we are going to allow Holy Spirit to uncover the lies that keep us hidden from God, much like Adam hid from God. Let us go into our hearing moment with open hearts. He will renew our minds and remind us that we are as His children, and we will become confident in His voice.

Hearing Moment

Write a letter to God. The only requirement is an open heart! What is keeping you from intimately knowing God? What questions do you have about Him? Holy Spirit will guide you out of hiding. Remember, God is not offended by your theories of Him. He already knows all and sees everything. He knows where you are, and He wants you to know that it is safe to be open with Him. As you write, be listening for that still, small voice that may answer questions, comfort you, and heal your heart. **Journal** everything down as He reveals Himself to you as you write your letter.

LESSON 2

FORGOTTEN IDENTITY

Digging Deeper

Read Genesis 3:1-5

It is important to note that Adam and Eve *did not* have a sin nature when they chose to disobey God. There was nothing of or in them that was lacking or depraved. That is why it is interesting that Satan deceived Eve by telling her to focus on what appeared to be lack. He had her focus on the only tree in the entire Garden from which she was not supposed to eat. He delivered his second blow by causing her to question God's motives and intentions for her life. In verses 4-5, Satan declared that Eve would not die if she ate the fruit and said God was trying to prevent her from becoming like Him. We all know that Adam and Eve were already created in the likeness and image of God. The Bible tells us so. Disobedience (sin), however, gave Adam and Eve the ability to view the world through the lens of death

1 Read the scripture posted below. Circle Eve's explanation for disobeying God.

In the Young's Literal Translation, which is a literal word-for-word translation, not a thought-for-thought translation, Eve confessed to God that the serpent caused her to forget! Eve forgot whom God was to her and that she was already like God. Can you imagine how God's heart was grieved for His children? Adam and Eve chose to disobey because they forgot who they were, and we all know those choices impacted all of us!

"And Jehovah God saith to the woman, 'What [is] this thou hast done?' and the woman saith, 'The serpent hath caused me to forget—and I do eat.'"
—Genesis 3:13, YLT

2 In your letter to God from Hearing Moment 1, you may have started to recognize Satan's tactics and listed ways you have mistrusted God. Are you able to see any of the same tactics Satan used on Eve in your own life? Are you making decisions in different areas of your life (relationships, parenting, finances, etc.) that are motivated by a forgotten identity? *Reflect* and *journal*.

Read Matthew 4:1-11

What does Scripture tell us about Jesus' behavior and His response to the devil's temptations?

The devil tempted Jesus, just as he tempted Eve in the Garden, by enticing Him to focus on what appeared to be lack and calling into question Jesus' identity. How did Jesus—who humbled Himself, became like man, and experienced every temptation we face today—not give in as Eve did? The devil searched and tried Jesus and found Jesus *knowing*, in faith, that He lacked nothing! Truth is never found lacking. Truth always conquers lies.

The devil found Jesus *resting* inside of faith and demonstrating the life we as believers are called to live. This faith comes from knowing who God is and who He says you are. This faith equips you to be obedient when the Holy Spirit leads you. This is how believers produce the fruit that the world recognizes is from God!

Jesus knew His Father, knew His identity, and because of His knowing He obediently trusted where Holy Spirit led Him. Jesus even proved that perfect circumstances are not what produce faith. Adam and Eve walked with God, had a lush green garden with abundant food, and they had authority and dominion, but they still made poor choices motivated by their forgotten identity. The Holy Spirit led Jesus into a wilderness, and He had no food for 40 days. Jesus' identity was rested *inside of God*, and He was able to *find His authority* to resist the killer, the stealer, the destroyer, the devil himself! Now that is a powerful reality that Jesus has given you!

> "Truly my soul finds rest in God; my salvation comes from him. Truly he is my rock and my salvation; he is my fortress, I will never be shaken."
> —Psalm 62:1-2

Does your faith in God cause you to rest in your knowledge of Him?

Be as transparent with yourself as possible. What or who does your faith rest in—yourself or someone else? Or does your faith rest in God's ability and the promises that come from your relationship with Him?

Complete the following sentences by filling in the blanks.

In the area of *finances* my faith is found resting in

_____

because I believe _____.

In the area of *relationship*s my faith is found resting in

_____ because I

believe _____.

In the area of *self-worth* my faith is found resting in

_____

because I believe_____.

In the area of *dreams* and careers my faith is found rest-

ing in _____ because

I believe _____.

Hearing Moment

It's time to remember who you are to God and what you look like in God! It's time that we take a good look through the eyes of Jesus and see ourselves the way He sees us.

If you have recognized that you have been living life from a forgotten identity, take a moment, acknowledge, and repent. Thank God for revealing the things that are keeping you from Him and that have been keeping you in hiding. It's time to walk in who you were always destined to be!

Next, ask Holy Spirit to show you how God sees you. Write down words you hear, sketch pictures that you see, and simply spend time acknowledging that what you are seeing and hearing is truth! Enjoy time in Abba's arms and testify of the goodness you have experienced with Him. Ask Him to give you a new "I am" statement. For example when I just asked, I heard, "I am *a solution*!"

LESSON 3

INSIDE OF HOPE

Digging Deeper

Ephesians 1 tells us that God planned in advance to be our Father before the world was formed. What does this say about God's heart toward humanity? We often view Adam and Eve's eviction from the Garden through the lens of an orphan who has been rejected by their Father, but I challenge you to open your heart and see God through a renewed mind.

Read Genesis 3:22. In this verse, God states man's problem: Adam and Eve's purity had been soiled. Their innocence was replaced with shame and a full knowledge of evil. God abruptly stopped speaking mid-sentence and *refused to speak of a fate that was never to be man's*! A fate of living eternally in a forgotten identity, robbed of purity, and conquered by unbelief.

"Then the Lord God said, 'Behold, the man has become like one of us in knowing good and evil. Now, lest he reach out his hand and take also of the tree of life and eat, and live forever—'"
—Genesis 3:22, ESV

Sometimes when we feel abandoned and defeated, we declare a future that fear has projected into our hearts and minds. It is important to note that God created everything in existence with words. If He refuses to speak of a potential reality that does not align with truth, then why are you prophesying death and destruction over the very life that God has given you and said was good? What do you believe in? Or better yet, whom do you believe in?

> Adam is not your point of origin, Christ is. Before Adam failed, Christ succeeded. If when you look in the rearview mirror of your existence you see Adam, look back further.
> —JEFF TURNER

God's hopes for creation never rested in mankind's ability to perform like Him. His hope was that humanity would place their faith in His likeness, from which they were created, and find dominion, be fruitful, and multiply.

"Once you were alienated from God
and were enemies in your minds because of your
evil behavior. But now he has reconciled you by Christ's
physical body through death to present you holy in his sight,
without blemish and free from accusation—if you continue
in your faith, established and firm, and do not move from
the hope held out in the gospel. This is the gospel that you
heard and that has been proclaimed to every creature under
heaven, and of which I, Paul, have become a servant."
—Colossians 1:21-23

Read Colossians 1:21-23 and respond.

1 According to verse 21, were you an enemy in God's mind or
in your mind?

2 Did God or man pursue and initiate reconciliation (see verse 22)?

3 In Jesus, we have been made *"holy in His sight."* In verse 22, *underline* what we are now free from and without!

4 What ways do you stay firmly established in your faith?

"I have become its servant by the commission
God gave me to present to you the word of God in its
fullness—the mystery that has been kept hidden for ages and
generations, but is now disclosed to the Lord's people. To them
God has chosen to make known among the Gentiles the glorious
riches of this mystery, which is Christ in you, the hope of glory."
—Colossians 1:25-27

Read Colossians 1:25-27 and respond.

5 According to verse 27, what is the mastery of the gospel?

6 In your opinion, why was the gospel message of Christ being *in* us worth Paul's lifelong devotion? What did this mean for all who heard it?

7 Strokes of God's nature are revealed through Paul's painting of the bigger picture of the gospel—we have placed our faith in Jesus Christ, so we have been reconciled to God and have been washed new. We are no longer enemies to God in our mind, because God has made it so that we can share in the glory of Jesus Christ. When you read these scriptures, what is God revealing about who He is?

"And this water symbolizes baptism
that now saves you also—not the removal of dirt
from the body but the pledge of a clear conscience toward
God. It saves you by the resurrection of Jesus Christ, who
has gone into heaven and is at God's right hand—with
angels, authorities and powers in submission to him."
—1 Peter 3:21-22

First Peter was a letter of encouragement written to the church. At the time it was written, being a follower of Christ meant abuse and persecution. Peter wanted to remind readers of where their hope was found. In light of this hope, they should all live holy lives testifying of the hope—Jesus Christ—that was found within them. Peter reminded them that it wasn't by the Old Covenant law that their hope was established; rather, hope was established by the New Covenant and the new creation that we have been baptized into through Jesus Christ. Peter's heart cry was for the church to live in and through the hope they had been given, though their circumstances were extremely hard!

In verse 21, Peter explained that baptism in Christ was not to wash the dirt from our physical bodies but to symbolize a pledge of what?

Proverbs 13:12 says, *"Hope deferred makes the heart sick, but a longing fulfilled is a tree of life."* In Jesus our hope has been fulfilled! He is the tree of life that has been offered to us, and we have taken from it! Accepting the gift of Christ has eternal consequences that begin today, not in some distant future! As Peter proclaimed, we are walking testimonies of Heaven on earth because of the hope that we abide in! As believers in Christ, reconciliation and righteousness are our possessions. We aren't looking for hope in external things, for our hope is found in Christ in us, the hope of glory! *Wow!* Thank You, Jesus!

Hearing Moment

As we read throughout the Bible, Jesus is our hope. He is truth! On the following page in your journal, draw a rectangle, and in the middle of that rectangle write the word *hope*.

1 Of the words listed below, pick out the ones that you connect with or that you hope for yourself, and write them inside the rectangle surrounding the word hope. Please add any other words that you feel accurately describe the identity and life you hope for today.

Supernatural	Dominion	Whole	Friendship
Authority	Peace	Faithful	Patience
Kindness	Joy	Self-Control	Gentleness
Love	Goodness	Freedom	Pure

2 Were there any words listed that you did not place inside your hope box? **Why?**

3 For each word listed inside your box of hope, write the direct opposite and place it outside of the perimeter of hope. Look at the example.

misery *joy*

HOPE

whole

broken

4 According to your rectangle of hope, living a life outside of hope has consequences. A life lived outside of hope is a life that is influenced by lies. Where you choose to live greatly influences your perception of life and persuades your choices. Are there areas of your life where you have no hope?

Do you identify your life more with what lives on the outside of hope? If so, then you are being influenced by lies! Allow Holy Spirit to lead you back into hope today, and take rest in Jesus! Take a moment and ask Holy Spirit to begin speaking hope back into your identity and life. List out the things about yourself or your life that appear to be hopeless. What is hope saying about it? Journal everything down and rest inside of hope again! Let your life testify about the hope you live in—Jesus Christ!

LESSON 4

A WHOLE NEW YOU

Digging Deeper

Read First Thessalonians 5:23-24.

Underline the three parts that make us a whole being.

Circle who it is who sanctifies us and keeps us holy.

> May God himself, the God of peace, sanctify you through and through. May your whole spirit, soul and body be kept blameless at the coming of our Lord Jesus Christ. The one who calls you is faithful, and he will do it.
> —1 Thessalonians 5:23-24

Understanding ourselves as a creation designed by God is an important step to embracing our identity as a new creation in Christ (see 2 Cor. 5:17). Most believers are comfortable with the idea that when we die, our natural body will go back into the dirt and the non-physical part of us will go to Heaven in a twinkling of eye, as is our promise as a believer (see 1 Cor. 15:52), but maybe not all of us exactly understand the three parts of us that Holy Spirit is renewing and sanctifying. Maybe we aren't exactly sure what *functioning whole* looks like. Some may not understand that we don't have to wait until we die and go to Heaven to walk out our new identity that can only be found in Christ!

Spirit

Greek word: *pneuma*—the wind, also breath (Strong's #G4151). The spirit is the invisible, non-physical part of man. It connects to God and is eternal (see Eccles. 12:7, 1 Cor. 5:3).

Soul

Greek word: *psyche*—breath of life (Strong's #G5590). The soul is the invisible, non-physical part of man. It contains the will, emotions, and thoughts of a man (Matt. 10:28, Rom. 2:9).

Body

Greek word: *soma*—body (Strong's #G4983). The body is a physical, tangible vessel that contains the non-physical parts of man. What you believe and agree with will be animated through your body (see Luke 12:4, 22).

Read Hebrews 4:12

Though you are one being, each part of you is being actively brought into wholeness and purity by the Word of God, Jesus Christ, which John clearly describes all throughout his gospel and letters.

> For the word of God is alive and active. Sharper than any double-edged sword, it penetrates even to dividing soul and spirit, joints and marrow; it judges the thoughts and attitudes of the heart.
> —Hebrews 4:12

The Word became flesh and made his dwelling among us. We have seen his glory, the glory of the one and only Son, who came from the Father, full of grace and truth (John 1:14).

One of Holy Spirit's beautiful pursuits is to reveal to you who Jesus is and what He has done for you. It's by grace, God's undeserved, unearned love, and by His supernatural power and truth that you are actively being transformed in your spirit and soul, which then manifests through your physical body. I have heard multiple testimonies of people receiving God's abundant love only to find they have been healed from a sickness or depression has left them. This is the beauty of Jesus' gift of salvation at work!

Let's explore our salvation and wholeness a little more!	
She will give birth to a son, and you are to give him the name Jesus, because he will save his people from their sins (Matthew 1:21).	And he said unto her, Daughter, be of good comfort: thy faith hath made thee whole; go in peace (Luke 8:48 KJV).
Both the word "save" in Matthew 1:21 and the word "whole" in Luke 8:48 mean the same thing.	

Salvation: *sozo* (Strong's #G4982)—to save, heal, recover, deliver, protect, preserve, to do well, and to be made whole (your entire human being).

Jesus came not only so that we could have eternal reconciliation with Abba but so that we would walk in supernatural and natural wholeness with God on earth in our whole being! Placing our faith in Jesus' accomplishments alone grants us Heaven's success on earth. We become victors, as Christ is victor! God's love is not just for one part of us; it's for our whole being. We are new and whole in Christ and we have been given eternal life with God, as mentioned in John 3:16. Let's take a closer look.

Eternal life: *aionies zoe* (Strong's #G166) refers to the miraculous perpetual life we simply receive upon believing—we can't earn it, we receive it.

Sozo is the whole package, and it comes by faith and trusting in the Word of God, Jesus, who is sanctifying us. Working out your salvation means your belief in the Word of God produces an action. It's not about striving to earn something from God. Your belief animates your life! What you see is what you become! Just like the woman Jesus told in Luke 8:48 to go in peace, Jesus told the man at the pool at Bethesda to pick up his mat and go (see John 5). Those who placed their faith in Jesus and received His grace and truth were forever changed; they believed, received, got up, and went! When we receive the gift of eternal life (*aionies zoe*) a life of wholeness (*sozo*) is ours to walk out by keeping our eyes on what He has done! His love leads us into freedom from sickness, all curses, poverty, death, and the list goes on. Your Bible is full of verses about the glory we receive in the gift of salvation, which is something you can't earn. (For further study on salvation versus eternal life I recommend *Heal Them All* by Cheryl Schang.)

> "Therefore, my dear friends, as you have always obeyed—not only in my presence, but now much more in my absence—continue to work out your salvation with fear and trembling."
> —Philippians 2:12

Hearing Moment

Therefore, if anyone is in Christ, the new creation has come: The old has gone, the new is here! (2 Corinthians 5:17)

Galatians 3:26-27 says, *"For you are all sons of God through faith in Christ Jesus. For all of you who were baptized into Christ have clothed yourselves with Christ"* (NASB). Through your belief in what Jesus died to give you, take a moment and imagine all three parts of you—spirit, soul, and body—receiving the fullness of salvation! Allow yourself to see the new creation that is you in Christ. Rest in the purity that has washed over your mind and that allows you to be unified and one with Him. There is no separation between you and Christ. Put on wholeness! Put on Christ.

If you have sickness in your body, take this moment to allow Jesus' love to touch that part and see it being made whole. Take this time and rest in wholeness. Simply *be* whole by receiving it by faith and not by trying to produce it or earn it.

journal

LESSON 5

EQUIPPED TO LIVE

And I will ask the Father, and he will give you
another Advocate, who will never leave you.
—JOHN 14:16, NLT

Digging Deeper

Down on my knees, frustrated with a powerless life and wondering if my prayers were even heard, I yelled and cried out to God for help—my life needed divine intervention. Interrupting my cries, a voice that I felt down in the marrow of my bones said, "Seek the Holy Spirit." As quickly as I heard, felt, experienced those words, my desperation was gone, my tears dried up, and my heart was full of incredible hope. Since meeting, knowing, and intentionally walking in relationship with Holy Spirit, my family and I walk out a lifestyle that is not only supernatural but also empowered and equipped. We are growing into the creation that God imagined in His heart— whole, free, and empowered!

In John 14:16, the word *advocate*, one of Holy Spirit's names, is translated from the Greek word *parakletos* and means to protect, defend, and save us from our self, our enemies, and keep us whole and healed (Strong's #G3875). Jesus died for us but more importantly was raised from the dead for us so that we would have life found in Him through life with Holy Spirit on earth. Holy Spirit isn't a thing. He is a person, a third member of the Godhead, and is dwelling with us and in us, guiding us into freedom, wholeness, and a supernaturally abundant life!

"Then the Lord God formed man from the dust of the ground and breathed into his nostrils the breath or spirit of life, and man became a living being."
—Genesis 2:7, AMPC

"Again Jesus said, 'Peace be with you! As the Father has sent me, I am sending you.' And with that he breathed on them and said, 'Receive the Holy Spirit.'"
—John 20:21-22

Read 1 Corinthians 15:45

When Jesus breathed on the disciples and said, *"Receive the Holy Spirit,"* He was fulfilling the prophecy of Ezekiel 11:19-20. In this significant act of breathing the Holy Spirit into man, Jesus totally obliterated sin's grip on our hearts and gave us back dominion over our lives. In Jesus, not only are we a new creation, we are reconciled to God and fully equipped to live in freedom through the guidance and empowerment of the Spirit of the living God within us! Regardless of current circumstances or your past, your stony heart has been made tender and alive and the Spirit enables your new heart to keep the law of love that has been written upon it. You have been radically made new and are equipped to change your world!

> "When you send your Spirit, they are created, and you renew the face of the ground."
> —Psalm 104:30

Scripture Work

In John 14:12-19 (AMPC) below, underline or highlight Jesus' declaration of what a believer's life should look like and how we have all been equipped.

I assure you, most solemnly I tell you, if anyone steadfastly believes in Me, he will himself be able to do the things that I do; and he will do even greater things than these, because I go to the Father.

And I will do [I Myself will grant] whatever you ask in My Name [as presenting all that I Am], so that the Father may be glorified and extolled in (through) the Son.

[Yes] I will grant [I Myself will do for you] whatever you shall ask in My Name [as presenting all that I Am].

If you [really] love Me, you will keep (obey) My commands.

And I will ask the Father, and He will give you another Comforter (Counselor, Helper, Intercessor, Advocate,

Strengthener, and Standby), that He may remain with you forever—

The Spirit of Truth, Whom the world cannot receive (welcome, take to its heart), because it does not see Him or know and recognize Him. But you know and recognize Him, for He lives with you [constantly] and will be in you.

I will not leave you as orphans [comfortless, desolate, bereaved, forlorn, helpless]; I will come [back] to you.

Just a little while now, and the world will not see Me any more, but you will see Me; because I live, you will live also.

You have been radically recreated with the breath of the living God. You have been equipped with everything necessary to live a life that isn't ordinary but, according to Jesus, is an extraordinary, supernatural life! The experiences you are having with Holy Spirit are the fulfillment of Jesus' promises that you would never be alone, that you would know Him, and that you would be equipped in this life to fulfill a destiny that you were designed for!

Hearing Moment

Think about the immeasurable amount of love that Abba Father, Jesus, and the Holy Spirit have for you. Think about the weighty worth you have that God would place Holy Spirit within and among you, so that you should be free and empowered! He wants you to experience that love and power!

Have you welcomed and taken to heart the presence of the Holy Spirit that resides within you?

Do you recognize the presence of the Spirit of Truth (Holy Spirit) that guides you into opportunities that renew your mind?

> "This is how God showed his love among us: He sent his one and only Son into the world that we might live through him. This is love: not that we loved God, but that he loved us."
> —1 John 4:9-10

First Corinthians 6:17 says that if we are united in Christ, we are one in Spirit with Him. Are you seeing how you are completely equipped and expected to engage Holy Spirit so that when you show up the world is forever impacted?

Take a moment, *close* your eyes if you would like, *open* your hands, and *ask* Holy Spirit to place a piece of equipment in your hands. It could be a tool, a piece of armor, or anything that Holy Spirit wants to give you so that you can become equipped to live an abundant life. Ask Him why He has given this specific item to you. *Journal* what it is you are receiving and why and how to apply this to your life so that you can begin to walk as an empowered believer.

LESSON 6

LIKE-MINDED LIFESTYLE

Do two walk together unless they
have agreed to do so?
—Amos 3:3

Digging Deeper

Every day you make choices that are based on belief and agreement. At this point in the study, we have learned the truth that God is pursuing us, we have practiced hearing His voice and understanding our identity as His child, and we have identified how to make choices from a place of righteousness and purity. We are living temples of Holy Spirit, who is leading us into incredible freedom when we agree with the incredible life He reveals to us (see 1 Cor. 2:16)! We have been set up to succeed because we not only know our Father but our life of faith reveals His great love to the world! Every day we are a manifestation of Heaven on earth!

Read John 5:19. Do you believe that God has given you the ability to know, see, and hear His ways, just as Jesus could? What are some ways Holy Spirit reveals God's desires for your life?

_____

_____

_____

_____

_____

_____

_____

_____

_____

Read John 5:20. What things did Jesus demonstrate that amaze you?

_____

_____

_____

_____

Read John 14. It's important that we get the picture that Jesus is painting clearly. In verse 7, whom did Jesus come to reveal?

In the Old Testament, God's chosen people proved over and over that they didn't know Him; they were terrified to even say

God's name. A construct was established, known as the Old Covenant, which kept the Israelites veiled from God's heart. God was mysterious, and they were unable to really know Him because they had been blinded by this covenant. As we know, this setup was not God's heart for His children, so He sent Jesus to establish a better covenant known as the New Covenant. Isaiah prophesied of the day when God's heart would finally be unveiled to the entire world. *"On this mountain he will destroy the shroud that enfolds all peoples, the sheet that covers all nations"* (Isa. 25:7). We know Isaiah was talking about Jesus!

Second Corinthians 3:15-16 says that even to this day when Moses's writings are read, a veil covers the heart of the Israelites so they do not understand God, but when they turn to Christ the veil is taken away. It is Jesus who came to reveal the Father and establish a covenant that leaves no question of the Father's amazing love for the world.

> "So all of us who have had that veil removed can see and reflect the glory of the Lord. And the Lord—who is the Spirit—makes us more and more like him as we are changed into his glorious image."
> —2 Corinthians 3:18, NLT

What Jesus was presenting was so radical to the Jews, not only because He identified Himself as from God and of God, but because He was calling God Father, revealing a side of God they had been blinded to! Their relationship with God had been based on performance and laws; they carried a great distance in their hearts and minds toward God. Thus, Jesus was considered heretical and dangerous! Jesus came to fulfill the requirements of the Old Covenant and establish a New Covenant that would be purely built on a love that not only forgave sin but transformed sinners into saints and is available to any who should receive it. This love empowers believers to live in unity and embrace a like-minded lifestyle with God, Jesus, and Holy Spirit. This love's atmosphere is called grace! It's what we breathe and exist in. Grace is equal parts undeserved love and power that transforms. In that environment, we walk in Heaven on earth as God's children and we reveal His likeness!

Like Jesus, we now can reveal to the world the Father's heart through power and love. Jesus set the standard of the lifestyle of the faith we profess today!

Once the Father affirmed Jesus' identity as His Son (see Matt. 3:17), Jesus began to walk out that belief, which demonstrated His agreement with what He saw His Father doing and heard His Father saying. Your belief is always saying yes to something, and because Jesus knew that He said this to us:

> *Very truly I tell you, whoever believes in me will do the works I have been doing, and they will do even greater things than these, because I am going to the Father* (John 14:12).

"They will do even greater things." Jesus wasn't talking about going back to works based off the law of the Old Covenant. He was talking about both the empowerment that comes from God's grace that we receive by faith, not performance, and God's undeserved love for us in that we are called His children. We have been empowered with a lifestyle in the New Covenant that is transformational to not only us but also to those who come in contact with us. We do because we can, because it's what we believe! It's who we are as God's children! Just as Jesus came to reveal

the Father, we are now revealing God by revealing His grace of power and undeserved love and demonstrating His nature and character to His children! This is the lifestyle of the New Covenant believer!

We know what happens next. Jesus' execution was plotted and carried out because of the revolutionary, exuberant lifestyle that Jesus proclaimed and demonstrated as God's child. Let's not miss the fact that God didn't force Jesus to die. It was Jesus' agreement with the Father's plan of establishing a better covenant through His Son's death and resurrection, and Jesus made this choice with freedom. Jesus wasn't mind-controlled by Holy Spirit, just as you aren't forced to live from your identity as a child of God either. It doesn't work that way. The Bible says that where the Spirit is there is freedom (see 2 Cor. 3:17). We know that to be free, one must have a choice.

Father, Son, and Holy Spirit worked together in perfect unity in their agreement to redeem mankind through God's perfect love with the New Covenant! Jesus' choice to die for us came from a belief in not only who He was and His purpose, but also because of how He felt about you and who you are to Him!

According to Ephesians 1:5-8 answer the following:

When did God (Father, Son, and Holy Spirit) decide to adopt us?

"God decided in advance to adopt us into his own family by bringing us to himself through Jesus Christ. This is what he wanted to do, and it gave him great pleasure. So we praise God for the glorious grace he has poured out on us who belong to his dear Son. He is so rich in kindness and grace that he purchased our freedom with the blood of his Son and forgave our sins. He has showered his kindness on us, along with all wisdom and understanding."
—Ephesians 1:5-8, NLT

How does knowing God chose you before you chose Him impact your belief about Him?

Jesus' blood has purchased our _____?

What fruit does your freedom produce? Is it life giving?

Grace (undeserved love and power that transforms us), kindness, *all* wisdom, and understanding has been showered upon us so that we can know God, agree with Him, and walk with Him. You have been chosen, built, and empowered to know and walk with God. Receiving this beautiful gift by faith will produce actions that come from our unity with Him, not a set of obligations and laws that veil God's heart. Your lifestyle reveals His nature, the character of the One you were created in the image of because you know Him, you see Him, you know His voice and His ways, and your belief in Him will produce this incredible life!

Are you ready for more out of life?

Hearing Moment

Close your eyes and give your heart the opportunity to use your imagination. Imagine the perfect piece of land. You don't know what it's used for or its purpose yet. Just imagine a perfect piece of property. Now design a perfect building that will be placed on that land. Using your *journal* below, draw and list out the attributes of the land and the building. Take notice of specific features, sizes, shapes, functions, and colors of your building and land.

For example:

> *I saw a mountaintop land with an incredible overview of a city below. The building I saw was a house. The house was an intelligent and stylish A-frame design, and was made of almost all glass to take advantage of the gorgeous views. It definitely made a statement to all those who saw it and could be seen from great distances.*

Complete the above step before reading on.

If you were the building and *the land was where God had placed you*—what does this say about you, how you function, how you are designed, and your purpose?

Journal down the connections you are making.

_____

_____

_____

_____

_____

_____

_____

_____

_____

_____

_____

_____

_____

_____

_____

_____

_____

God was showing me, for example, that I was positioned in a restful place that would be a beacon of hope (light that can be seen at quite a distance) and that I have security (by design and placement), authority (strategic views), and provision (high-priced real estate). I was not only to be seen but had a voice to be heard. I would be attracting people upward and into great heights with Him. And the fact that the house was made of all glass spoke of my very transparent nature and willingness to expose my heart.

James 1:5 says that anyone who lacks wisdom should just ask and it shall be given. Just as Ephesians 1:5-8 states, God has lavished all of His wisdom and understanding on us.

Take this opportunity to not only hear what God is saying about who you are, where you have been placed, and how you function in that environment, but allow it to become wisdom that activates your beliefs. Do your part in partaking in like-mindedness with Christ and walk out that reality. Choices rooted in God's abundant wisdom can change not only your current circumstances but also your life if you would simply agree and believe!

Journal

LESSON 7

YOU WILL BE KNOWN

All glorious is the princess within her chamber;
her gown is interwoven with gold. In embroidered
garments she is led to the king.... I will perpetuate
your memory through all generations; therefore
the nations will praise you for ever and ever.
—Psalm 45:13-14, 17

Digging Deeper

Read Genesis 3:21

What is the first thing God does for Adam and Eve before they
are removed from the Garden of Eden?

Like a good Father, God calls Adam and Eve out and He clothes them, covering their nakedness and shame. This illustrates a beautiful picture of God's heart toward man and points toward the day when His Son Jesus Christ would call us out and clothe us!

Circle the *garments* and the *robe* Isaiah prophesied Jesus would clothes us in, according to Isaiah 61:10.

As the bride of Christ, you are clothed in the most expensive garments on earth and in Heaven. **Wow!**

Jesus says in John 5:19 that He only does what He sees His Father doing. God foreshadowed the immense love and mercy that He would demonstrate for us through His Son Jesus Christ when He clothed Adam and Eve and covered their nakedness and shame.

> "I delight greatly in the Lord; my soul rejoices in my God. For he has clothed me with garments of salvation and arrayed me in a robe of his righteousness, as a bridegroom adorns his head like a priest, and as a bride adorns herself with her jewels."
> —Isaiah 61:10

Read John 17:20-23

What is it that Jesus has given us so that what should be known?

John records an intimate prayer from Jesus to God the Father: *"I have given them the glory that you have given me."* The word *glory* in this scripture is *doxa* in the Greek, and is defined as a weighty honor, favorable opinion, and also a shining majesty that comes from being in the presence of God (Strong's #G1391).

We have been clothed in royal garments of love and will be known by the honor that God has placed on our life. In our relationship with God, His face shines upon us and reflects the glory of His majesty, revealing His Kingdom in which we belong.

Jesus said in John 17:4 that He brought glory to God by completing the work He had set out to do, which was revealing the Father to the world so that man should have eternal life. By establishing a New Covenant through His death and resurrection, humanity is now set free and unveiled so we can all see and reflect the glory of God.

God will make you known so that when you shine the world will see His love, grace, mercy, and goodness. You have received freely all of Him by faith through the trust that comes from believing! God has placed you in His righteousness because He knew you before you knew Him. He believed in your potential before you even knew you had any. You were found worthy while still in your worthlessness.

We didn't earn God's favor; it was given when we believed and received it. When we came to Christ we handed in our filthy rags for His robes of righteousness. We traded shame for the honor that He so freely gave us. But it's Satan who comes to deceive you and blind you to who you are and to the righteousness with which you have been clothed.

Reflect on Second Corinthians 4:4

Highlight what stands out to you. Make notes of connections learned throughout the previous lessons and hearing moments.

> *Satan, who is the god of this world, has blinded the minds of those who don't believe. They are unable to see the glorious light of the Good News. They don't understand this message about the glory of Christ, who is the exact likeness of God* (2 Corinthians 4:4 NLT).

In your opinion, can a "Christian" be an unbeliever?

As we learned in "Lesson 2: Forgotten Identity," like Eve we can encounter God, but we can become blinded orphans who don't truly believe in the glory that Jesus has shared with us when we try to achieve what has already been freely given to us. We walk around in royal attire that identifies us with a King who has shared everything with us, but we act like orphans who still beg because we are blinded to who we are. We beg for God's presence, yet Jesus has placed us in His throne room where we stand shining in God's likeness, embraced by His secure arms. God is calling us into knowing Him through His Son Jesus Christ so that we may be known as He is known. John 12:45 says that when you look into the face of Jesus you are looking into the face of the Father. When we look, we find love! Jesus said:

> *A new commandment I give to you, that you love one another, even as I have loved you, that you also love one another. By this all men will know that you are My disciples, if you have love for one another* (John 13:34-35 NASB).

He was speaking about the only law that the New Covenant is centered around—the law of love. Love has covered everything. It covers your past, your present, and your future. It equips you to surpass all limitations. It gives you the permission and the freedom to throw down laws of old and embrace something more powerful—a love that inspires revelation and dreams. This love gives you vision that comes from knowing who you are because you have placed your faith in the One who has always known you.

Without faith in this love that Jesus has revealed and established permanently through the New Covenant, you cannot share in the glory because it's not something you can achieve; you simply receive. The word *faith* can be defined as a trustful response that comes from knowing God. The Hebrew word is *aman* and it means reliable, stable, to uphold as a father who upholds a child would (Strong's #H539). Faith is built upon the promise of a Father who always keeps His word. God has established a covenant of love that He cannot break. He can only honor this covenant, and He continues to honor it with us. It is by our faith (a trust that comes from knowing God) in what Jesus has done that we freely receive this gift of glory and enter into oneness with God, just as Jesus and the Father are one, and then we shine for all to see.

Let's continue our reading of Second Corinthians 4. Hear what Paul is saying:

> *You see, we don't go around preaching about ourselves. We preach that Jesus Christ is Lord, and we ourselves are your servants for Jesus' sake. For God, who said, "Let there be light in the darkness," has made this light shine in our hearts so we could* **know** *the glory of God that is seen in the face of Jesus Christ* (2 Corinthians 4:5-6 NLT).

All the striving is done. He will make you known through your faith. You were destined to have a glorious life because it reveals the glory of God that has been given to us. God uncovers the real you, and by you being uniquely you God's light shines forth and manifests His glory.

Hearing Moment

God sees you sparkling in salvation and standing in a robe of righteousness. You, child of God, are royalty. You are wearing the most expensive attire—the blood of Jesus Christ. Your destiny was always designed with Jesus Christ in mind, and you are wired to shine in the glory He's placed on your life.

Jesus Himself has called you the light of the world because you are unified with the Light of the World—Jesus. In God's grace (undeserved love and power) we were made to shine. Through God's favor

"You are the light of the world. A town built on a hill cannot be hidden. Neither do people light a lamp and put it under a bowl. Instead they put it on its stand, and it gives light to everyone in the house. In the same way, let your light shine before others, that they may see your good deeds and glorify your Father in heaven."
—Matthew 5:14-16

we are empowered to succeed. We can't earn it, but by faith (trust in God's word) we receive it and live it.

Close your eyes and see yourself standing in His light. Holy Spirit will reveal God clothing you in garments of salvation and robes of righteousness. *Journal* what you are seeing and hearing.

Next, I want you see yourself receiving the glory (weighty honor) that God has placed on your life. If you struggle with the lie of worthlessness, understand He has found you worthy enough to drape you in His Son's blood. Receive His grace so that you can accept His abundant love. It is undoubtedly hard to receive His great love that we didn't earn, but His Word and His promise are being fulfilled through the New Covenant that Jesus has given us. You may hear words in your heart or see images in your mind. Draw or write everything He shares with you.

Remember, you were designed to hear and see God. *Journal* your first impressions and just simply be God's child with your heart set to hear Him.

LESSON 8

LEAVING A LEGACY

A good man leaves an inheritance
to his children's children.
—Proverbs 13:22, NASB

Digging Deeper

If you read through the different covenants (oath-bound promises God had with man) throughout the Bible, we see that God consistently described those He was in covenant with as His very own inheritance. God receives us as His own inheritance. Think about that. You have so much value and importance that God considers you His very own inheritance.

Moses, as well as others whom God told, tried to explain this reality to the Israelites, who lived during what is known as the Mosaic covenant. This inheritance type of language can be seen repeatedly all throughout the cannon that surrounds the Mosaic covenant.

"For you are a holy people, who belong to the Lord your God. Of all the people on earth, the Lord your God has chosen you to be his own special treasure. The Lord did not set his heart on you and choose you because you were more numerous than other nations, for you were the smallest of all nations! Rather, it was simply that the Lord loves you, and he was keeping the oath he had sworn to your ancestors."
—Deuteronomy 7:6-8, NLT

Read Deuteronomy 7:6-8

Why do you think Moses pointed out that God's devotion to them had nothing to do with numbers but everything to do with love and promises kept?

The Israelites, who had been heavily oppressed in dry, hot Egypt, a land that was described in First Kings 8:51 as an "iron-smelting furnace," struggled breaking free from a slave mindset—a perspective that had been passed down to their children's children throughout the 400 years they were in captivity.

God diligently reminded them of their identity as His inheritance, a chosen people, and He reminded them of the promises that they were to inherit—a land flowing with milk and honey. This land represented abundance, success, and permission to live as free people of God. In all of this, God encouraged them to place their faith in His strong hands, because He honors and protects those He loves, His very own inheritance.

Many of us know the story of the Israelites, and we may even identify with them at times. They have been described as stiff-necked, stubborn people who easily forgot. But because we place our faith in who we are in Christ and in the better covenant that God established, as discussed in Lesson 6, we are co-heirs of a legacy that will be passed down throughout the generations through our faith.

"My choice is you, God, first and only. And now I find I'm your choice! You set me up with a house and yard. And then you made me your heir! The wise counsel God gives when I'm awake is confirmed by my sleeping heart. Day and night I'll stick with God; I have got a good thing going and I'm not letting go. I'm happy from the inside out, and from the outside in, I'm firmly formed. You canceled my ticket to hell—that's not my destination! Now you've got my feet on the life path, all radiant from the shining of your face. Ever since you took my hand, I'm on the right way."
—Psalm 16:5-11, MSG

Read Psalm 16:5-11

Circle the passage where David speaks of God giving him a domain of his own.

Just like Adam in the Garden was in charge of naming the animals and overseeing the entire Garden, God gives us all areas of influence in which to spend our inheritance of authority, joy, and victory. Through our faith in what Christ has done and who we are in Him, we use our freedom in Christ to serve those around us by revealing the likeness of our good, good Father and bringing victory into areas of need. Being successful, innovative, and creative demonstrates God's glory that He releases to us through our faith. List out the realms of influence in every area of life in which God's given you influence. There is no area too small or too big:

_____

_____

_____

_____

_____

_____

_____

_____

_____

David says that he is happy from the inside out and the outside in and is firmly formed by God. Imagine your life with that kind of security and confidence all wrapped up in joy! As David mentioned in the psalm above, Abba gives you wise counsel during the day and confirms it at night so that you know He's guiding you.

Read Hebrews 12:2. What does the scripture say was set before Jesus as the reason He endured the cross?

_____

_____

_____

_____

_____

Psalm 2:7-8 says, *"The Lord said to me, 'You are my son. Today I have become your Father. Only ask, and I will give you the nations as your inheritance, the whole earth as your possession'"* (NLT). David prophetically sang of all the nations being Jesus' inheritance. Just as Hebrews 12:2 says, Jesus endured the cross to receive the joy that was set before Him—an inheritance of the nations that includes you!

Once we have realized that Jesus has brought us into this incredible family and made us a co-heir (see Acts 20:32), we then understand that Jesus' inheritance of the nations is now ours! Adam and Eve inherited the earth, but God started them off with a smaller domain known as the Garden. As we have learned, they placed their faith outside of God, forgetting who God was and who they were. By placing our faith in God, we can see ourselves how He sees us. Because we know Him, we can trust in the dreams and the desires of our hearts. We are learning that God placed those dreams and desires within us so that we could learn how to be His children and live as free people who are victorious, just as our King Jesus is. We are no longer orphans. We are no longer slaves. We are children of God! The legacy that you will leave for the generations to come will be found in the promises God whispers in your ears and in the plans He shows your heart. The inheritance that He has given you will be manifested through your very unique dreams and desires. Christ has given you permission to live and have an abundant life!

As we know Heaven is our inheritance, we also must know that God gave us the earth to have dominion over. God is a giver. This is who He is, and He gives so that you can be empowered and free!

> "For [even the whole] creation (all nature) waits expectantly and longs earnestly for God's sons to be made known [waits for the revealing, the disclosing of their sonship]."
> —Romans 8:19, AMPC

Read Romans 8:19

Do you believe you have a purpose on this earth? Jesus Christ, the solution to every problem in the world, lives within you. What void in the earth is waiting for you to show up and fill it? When you dream of serving, helping, being a solution—what do you see? What pulls at your heart? Are inventions resting within your heart that you have not touched? Are new businesses that could create jobs and wealth for the Kingdom lying dormant in your mind? *Journal* the first thoughts that pop into your heart. There's no need to overthink it.

The world needs to experience the fruit of your union with God, your sonship, and to see this fruit manifested in the earth. Every area of your life is groaning for you to reveal your true identity, an identity that has been forgiven, made pure, given a right mind and spirit, and is victorious over everything because King Jesus has overcome the world (see John 16:33). Start by revealing that identity in what's right in front of you—relationships, home, money, time, health, and so on.

What areas of your life need you, a child of God, to show up? Where can the power of forgiveness, self-control, or creative solutions be applied in your life? Let go of offenses, make choices from grace and truth, and reveal the fruit of the Spirit. Allow Holy Spirit to show you areas of your life that need you to display the grace and truth that has been given to you. *Journal* what He reveals to you.

Children of God, we carry within us a knowledge that surpasses human reasoning. Our lives are a sweet fragrance as we live out this triumphant identity in Christ and are led by God. We will be known by our faith and by the love that has been lavished upon us by our good Father.

We have a good King who reigns and who has seated us with Him in heavenly places (see Eph. 2:6). He has given us every spiritual blessing in Heaven so that we can reign on earth and demonstrate the Kingdom of God everywhere we go. Our legacies will be carried out as we live out our dreams and pass our faith on to our children and the next generation. As you wake up and respond to the calling on your life, the world will want to know who you are, and you will say, "I am my Father's child, a child of God!"

"Therefore, since we have so great a cloud of witnesses surrounding us, let us also lay aside every encumbrance and the sin which so easily entangles us, and let us run with endurance the race that is set before us, fixing our eyes on Jesus, the author and perfecter of faith...."
—Hebrews 12:1-2 NASB

Hearing Moment

You are a child of God with promises spoken over you before you were even born. You were designed to reign with Christ.

> But you are a chosen people, a royal priesthood, a holy nation, God's special possession, that you may declare the praises of him who called you out of darkness into his wonderful light.
> —1 Peter 2:9

Let's take a moment and allow Holy Spirit to speak promises over our lives and our future.

Pray and ask Holy Spirit to share and show you the promises that God has set before you. You may hear one or several. *Journal* everything you hear and see. With each promise you receive, ask Holy Spirit for practical first steps to begin walking in faith toward that promise.

_____

_____

_____

_____

_____

_____

_____

_____

_____

I AM REFLECTION

In the Gospel of John, Jesus responds to the question "Who am I?" with what are called the I AM statements of Jesus. All throughout the gospels, we find Jesus revealing and demonstrating these I AM statements, proving He was more than just a teacher or a prophet. He was I AM.

God first introduced Himself to Moses as I AM—the one who was, is, and always will be (see Exod. 3:13-15). No other teacher ever dared to claim they were of God, from God, and with God as Jesus did in John 8:58. Jesus, identifying Himself as I AM, claimed to exist even before Abraham, the father of the Jewish faith. Jesus also claimed to be equal with God, to co-exist with Him, and to be co-eternal with God, who is the Father of all of creation.

These statements ultimately brought about Jesus' death. His death and resurrection permanently impacted our identity. We have died with Christ and have risen with Him as new creations, and our very own I am's have changed. Because of that truth, we step onto a path that is paved with promises and bound for glory.

As we come to a close in this devotional, take some time and read Jesus' I AM statements found in the scriptures posted below. *Journal* down what Holy Spirit reveals to you.

Jesus' **I AM** statements in John's Gospel:

"**I am** the bread of life" (6:35,41,48-51).

"**I am** the light of the world" (8:12; 9:5).

"**I AM**" (8:58).

"**I am** the door of the sheep" (10:7,9).

"**I am** the good shepherd" (10:11,14).

"**I am** the resurrection and the life" (11:25).

"**I am** the way and the truth and the life" (14:6).

"**I am** the true vine" (15:1,5).

It's vital to see that Jesus never denied who He was, even though He demonstrated great humility and servanthood. The King of Heaven and earth offered Himself as a gift to the world. Jesus' power was secure in His Father's validation and not in man's approval. He let go of anything He was entitled to so that He could become a gift to the world from the Father. Because of who He was, Jesus was able to redeem everything, and He made all things new and He leads His believers into freedom.

According to Jesus' I AM declarations, did Jesus identify Himself as an entitled King or as a servant to all those who believed in Him?

Read Philippians 2:6-11. Do you know the difference between false humility and true humility? Explain.

Take a moment to read through each **Digging Deeper** lesson and **Hearing Moment** and write out "I am" statements based on what God declared over you and the experiences you had with Him in your hearing moments. Record them below. Hopefully, you find at least one per lesson, if not more.

Just as Jesus' I AM statements revealed who He was, they also express promises to those who should believe. Your identity is not only who God says you are, but your identity as a son or daughter of God includes an invitation to enter into a life of promises, favor, and glory that is empowered by God's grace.

Jesus understood that He was a promise being fulfilled. The miracles He performed were specific and deliberate. All those watching Jesus knew He was identifying Himself as the fulfillment of prophetic promises from God that had been declared by the prophets of old. Some believed and some rejected Him because they wanted their King to be different. Some wanted something more impressive, not realizing that a King who served was unlike anything the world had ever seen before.

In your identity are promises waiting to be unlocked. We receive by faith that Jesus has made us new, and from that truth we are empowered to leave a legacy for future generations. Jesus said in John 14:6, *"I am the way and the truth and the life."* Jesus was revealing that He would lead all those who believed into all righteousness, into all wisdom, and into an abundant life. As you come into agreement with and fully believe in the I am statements God has given you, you will begin to walk in the fulfillment of these promises.

Write the I am statements you pulled from each lesson below, and allow Holy Spirit to reveal to you the promise that comes with each statement. For example: During a hearing moment Holy Spirit may have shown you singing. The I am statement I would pull from that, especially if you have a gift of singing that you are maybe afraid to use, is "I am a singer." The promise I'd pull from that I am statement is that God will give me opportunities to use my voice and His grace to do it.

"I am" Statements	Promises that are attached to this "I am" declaration

journal

journal

ABOUT BETSY JACOBS

Betsy Jacobs is a writer, speaker, and life consultant/development coach. Her devotional study is used by small groups and individuals from around the world, and her coaching practice has allowed her to pastor individuals from all walks of life. She's taught in online prophetic schools, produced prophetic curriculum, and equipped the church in hearing God's voice for over a decade. Her husband Ben and their two sons, Jake and Jackson, are known as a family who walk with God, Who has planted them, for now, in Springfield, Missouri.

Learn more about Betsy at www.exuberantliferevolution.org.